Edited by Ann
and James Do

Is there anyone here
from education?

Pluto Press

Acknowledgements

This book has been produced at a speed which would not have been possible without the support and collaboration of many people. We would especially like to thank Fred Halliday, for his enthusiasm and encouragement in the early stages; all the contributors, who kept (more or less) to deadlines which put them under considerable pressure; Lorraine Belam, for an unjustifiable amount of secretarial help; and the people at Pluto, particularly Richard Kuper, who combined commitment with efficiency to rush through the production process.

First published in 1983 by Pluto Press Limited,
The Works, 105a Torriano Avenue, London NW5 2RX and
Pluto Press Australia Limited, PO Box 199, Leichardt,
New South Wales 2040, Australia

Copyright © Pluto Press, 1983
Articles copyright © the individual author(s), 1983

Set by Grassroots, 101 Kilburn Square, London NW6
Printed in Great Britain by Photobooks Ltd, Bristol
Bound by W.H. Ware Ltd. Clevedon, Avon

British Library Cataloguing in Publication Data
   Is there anyone here from education?
    1. Education and state—Great Britain
    I. Wolpe, AnnMarie   II. Donald, James
    379.41   LC93.G7

ISBN 0-86104-736-2

Contents

Part three: Terms of debate

Part four: Teachers, parents and students

List of abbreviations

AMMA	Assistant Masters and Mistresses' Association
APS	Assisted Places Scheme
APU	Assessment of Performance Unit
AUT	Association of University Teachers
CBI	Confederation of British Industry
CSE	Certificate of Secondary Education
DES	Department of Education and Science
FE	Further education
GCE	General Certificate of Education
HE	Higher education
HMI	Her Majesty's Inspectorate
ILEA	Inner London Education Authority
LEA	Local Education Authority
MSC	Manpower Services Commission
NAB	National Advisory Board
NAS/UWT	National Association of Schoolmasters/Union of Women Teachers
NATFHE	National Association of Teachers in Further and Higher Education
NTI	New Training Initiative
NUT	National Union of Teachers
PAT	Professional Association of Teachers
PSBR	Public sector borrowing requirement
PTA	Parent Teacher Association
TES	*Times Educational Supplement*
THES	*Times Higher Educational Supplement*
TVEI	Technical and Vocational Education Initiative
WEEP	Work Experience in Employers' Premises
YOP	Youth Opportunity Programme
YTS	Youth Training Scheme

Introduction

When the votes had all been counted on 10 June 1983, and Margaret Thatcher confirmed in Downing Street, the British electorate had chosen 5 more years of a government which had run down the state education system to an unprecedented degree. Whether this deterioration had happened by design or merely through malign neglect and incompetence should now become more clear — even Margaret Thatcher was reportedly moved to describe the consequences of educational policy during her first term as 'a disaster'.

This book was conceived and written in the run-up to that election. It is a response to a particular feature of it: the striking absence of any serious discussion about education. Given their record, such discretion on the part of the Tories is easily understood. Their most notable contribution to the debate was Norman Tebbit's remark that 'we've taken the money away from the people who write about ancient Egyptian scripts and the pre-nuptial habits of the Upper Volta Valley.' (This at least clarified that industrial relevance rather than academic excellence is now the number-one priority.) More surprising was the lack of an effective polemical response from the left. The Labour Party attacked cuts in education, along with the decline of welfare provision in general, and pushed its traditional policy of extending access — this time mainly to post-18 education. But given the earlier centrality of education to Labour's strategies for social transformation, why should it now have so little positive to say on the question?

Free, universal secondary education was established in Britain by R.A.Butler's 1944 Education Act. It was part of the post-war political settlement in which the state, in line with Keynesian thinking, took a more àctive role in managing the economy and also in meeting popular demands for social services through the welfare state.

Education therefore had a dual role. Working-class voters were being told that their problem was the lack of equal opportunities, created by a class-divided society. Industrialists were being told that a skilled workforce was a prerequisite for industrial efficiency and economic growth. And both were being told that the solution was education. This apparent community of interests around education never really hid the fact that these two commitments were pulling in different directions — the first towards greater egalitarianism (through the introduction of comprehensive schooling, for example) and the second towards greater selection and differentiation (through the maintenance of an examination system that guarantees the 'failure' of most children, for example).

This tension could be managed as long as the economy continued to prosper and, despite heated skirmishes over such issues as comprehensive schooling, both Conservative and Labour governments shared a commitment to the extension of education. But as the long post-war boom slowed down during the 1960s and juddered into reverse in the 1970s, the educational consensus began to crack. Buying popular political support through welfare provision became too expensive as domestic inflation soared and the global recession deepened. In the mid-1970s, Denis Healey, then the Labour Chancellor of the Exchequer, was blinded by the monetarist light on the road to the International Monetary Fund. The cycle of ever deeper cuts in expenditure on education began.

At the same time, the commonsense assumption that education was a good thing both for individuals and for the nation was being called into question. An ideological offensive had been launched in the late 1960s by right-wing academics: its flagship was the series of so-called Black Papers which attacked what they considered a corrosive ethos of egalitarianism. To begin with, they were widely dismissed as a heretical backlash. But by the time the Labour Prime Minister James Callaghan launched his Great Debate on education in 1976, the terms of reference were almost entirely those of the radical right. True, the question of academic excellence took second place to making education serve the 'needs of industry' more closely, but this change of emphasis was also visible in the Black Papers which Rhodes Boyson co-edited in the mid-1970s. The right-wing press — notably the *Daily Mail*, *Express* and *Sun* — also joined in gleefully.

They attacked declining standards and indiscipline, attributed to 'trendy' 'left-wing' teachers and exploited cases like the row over William Tyndale School in their campaign against 'progressivism'.

These attacks on state education were successful because they did tap some genuine popular perceptions and grievances. Far from engineering any significant social or economic change, compulsory secondary schooling, even comprehensive schooling, had signally failed to correct existing patterns of educational inequality. The form in which it was provided could also make it an alienating experience. Parents might feel excluded from any say in the conduct or control of education — the Tories picked up on this and made 'parental choice' the central plank of their educational platform for the 1979 election. The changes in the institutional form of schooling were not accompanied by a thoroughgoing reassessment of the appropriate curriculum content, and so many pupils have felt excluded from the cultural values it embodies. In a period of mass youth unemployment, the route through educational qualifications to higher education or a well-paid job — always a narrow one — can seem impassable. Paradoxically, though, the old idea that education should provide individual qualifications or skills which can improve the chances of employment — the traditional view of the educational marketplace — reasserts itself all the more strongly when the competition for work becomes more intense.

Fears about the social dangers posed by long-term youth unemployment were as influential in shaping the Callaghan government's reforms as the standard complaints from employers about innumeracy and illiteracy among school leavers. The mid-1970s saw a substantial shift not only of emphasis but also of resources from general education to vocational preparation — the latter designed to inculcate appropriate attitudes in the absence of jobs through which 'work discipline' would normally have been learnt. This change required the restructuring of the state's machinery for the administration of education. The mandarins of the Department of Education and Science were by-passed by the generously funded Manpower Services Commission, which answers to the Minister of Employment and is designed to gear the education system to the management and control of the workforce.

It was in such ways that the Callaghan government prepared the ground for the Thatcherite offensive charted in Part One of this book. When it eventually faced up to the problems and inadequacies which undeniably existed within the state system, the tragedy is that the Labour Party in power did so from a conservative perspective and came up with conservative solutions. Even the *idea* that education might have purposes other than serving the needs of industry was off the agenda.

Undoubtedly the prospect over the next few years is gloomy. Part of the problem, it has to be admitted, is that, having jettisoned education as a means of social change in favour of using it to contain the problem of unemployment, the Labour Party goes on talking as if nothing had changed. The need to develop a coherent new strategy for education is part of the broader problem now facing the left. This is well expressed by Stuart Hall and Martin Jacques in their introduction to *The Politics of Thatcherism*:

> The question is whether a credible, alternative political force can be constructed equal to the historic tasks which confront the country at this juncture and capable of matching Thatcherism on the many fronts on which it has engaged. In that context, Thatcherism is a problem, not just 'for' the left, but *of* the left. Its rise was predicated on Labour's decline. It seized on precisely those points of popular consciousness which Labourism had abandoned. It exploited the internal contradictions which the social democratic corporatist strategy of successive Labour governments had generated ... Thatcherism did not advance into an empty space. It invaded and seized territory from a Labourism which had lost its popular-democratic connections and which appeared increasingly as, simply, a less and less efficient or convincing manager of capitalist crisis.

So what is required in this political context is a fundamental transformation of the left in Britain, a rethinking of its strategies and policies from first principles. That does not mean that there should be any question about its commitment to the provision of free, universal schooling by the state. Nor is it a call for utopian educational blueprints. What it will involve is a detailed, critical examination of the forms in which education is provided and what it can actually be expected to achieve. No false promises, in other words, but an explicit attempt to establish the proper role of education in the management of the economy by a Labour government and also the real extent of social change that can be achieved through education. This will entail a thoroughgoing reconsideration of the culture produced through the curriculum and pedagogy of the schools, and the social divisions they sustain. The extension of access to education and changes in the institutional forms of schooling, necessary as they are, cannot bring about any significant change unless they take account of these broader cultural and social questions.

This book is an early contribution to the process of reconstruction — very much some first thoughts rather than the last word. It does not pretend to cover all aspects of education, nor do the contributors agree by any means on all issues. They are suggesting questions that socialists and feminists ought now to be asking themselves, and terms of debate which can lead to new analyses and new strategies. Their differences of emphasis and approach are therefore valuable. They indicate the rejection of old clichés and easy solutions. Instead, they set out a range of possibilities which may open up new ways forward. They do not constitute a line or a blueprint to be imposed from above. The construction of a new strategy must involve those whom it will affect. In the first instance, this may mean forging alliances at the local level around limited, often defensive objectives — alliances between groups like parents, teachers and students whose interests may now seem to conflict. But this should also include — not as an optional extra in the longer term, but as a matter of urgent practical politics and pedagogic practice — working through the question of what it would actually mean to make schooling democratic and accountable. Only through the mobilization of popular democratic support around issues such as education can the left be renewed and transformed. And that is how Thatcherism will be defeated.

Part one

The politics of education

1. Education in crisis

Stuart Hall

Education in Britain has entered a deep crisis. It is, in fact, a *double* crisis — for there is little point in pretending that all was right, say, with the comprehensive school until Margaret Thatcher's government appeared on the scene. The first aspect of the crisis arises from the fact that Labour's historic programme in education, which spanned the post-war period, and can be summed up under the banner of 'universal provision' or 'comprehensivization', has reached some sort of terminal point. It marked a significant watershed in the advance towards equality of opportunity in education. But it is no longer adequate to the problems which have emerged over the past two decades and it is no longer a force around which popular forces are mobilizing. Nor does it inspire and generate fresh thinking. It has run out of steam, and there is nothing yet to replace it. It cannot do what it did four decades ago — dominate educational thinking.

That is challenge enough for the left. But as if it were not serious enough, this closure has been matched by the opening of one of the most regressive educational offensives ever unwrapped in this century. This is the other side of the crisis — Margaret Thatcher's 'modest proposal' to drive the educational bandwagon as rapidly as possible back to the stone age. The short-term cuts and savaging of the system that are actually going on are written large for anyone on the run to read. But we should not underestimate the strategic, long-term thinking or the coherence of the philosophical inspiration which now animates the educational programme of the 'radical right'. As in many other departments of social life, the object is nothing short of dismantling a whole epoch, reversing the fundamental directions, disorganizing the field and inaugurating a new era. Privatization is intended to erode the very principle of state provision. The standards being aspired to as required to take Britain into the twentieth century are those of the

Victorian board school. The concern with the dress, deportment and manicured voices of teachers is aimed at turning back the tide of progressive thinking and practice and the restoration of *social*, not educational, authority and discipline *through* the classroom. The fate of nursery education is not simply a side-effect of 'cash limits' and cuts in public spending. It is intended to underpin the confinement of women to hearth and home, to cut off the tide of their independence and to discourage any temptation to forsake their 'natural' destiny. The brutal revival of vocationalism in its most reductive form and the division of the world forever into 'hands' and 'brains', each with its appropriate slot in the educational structure, corresponds to a general vision of class domination. Inequality in education has become, once again, a *positive* social programme. And it flows from and underpins a vision of the future, sordid and degraded as it is.

The problem is that it is not matched on the other side by any corresponding vision. And the awkward truth is that, though the remedies offered are desperate for the mass of ordinary working people in this country, the problems at which they are aimed are not illusory. In education as elsewhere, the radical right has advanced by engaging the real weak points and exploiting the contradictions of the left. And it is because the right really has exposed some of the contradictions of the system — even if only to construct and deform it into their own reactionary line — that we cannot afford to ignore their starting-points. The crisis is not only of *their* making. It is *ours* too.

The great dividing line on which Labour's educational programme was based was drawn around the opposition to educational privilege: education as a universal right, like other welfare benefits — the concept of a comprehensive schooling available for all classes. But, in political terms, that is really as far as it went. It attended to the machinery of reform — the comprehensive school — but not to its actual conditions of existence, its real practices and strategic social purposes. Fabian-like, it assumed that all these 'details' were best left to the experts and professionals. Believing ultimately in the neutrality of the state, Labour does seem to have subscribed to the erroneous view that 'Education should really be taken out of politics.' It is not an error Margaret Thatcher's government is likely to make. They know only too well that a vision of what British society should look like in the future is incapable of mobilizing populist support or being realized without a 'politics of education'. Consequently, though comprehensive schooling marked a significant turning-point, it has not stemmed the tide of educational competition. There has been no fresh mobilization around it, no deepening of its democratic content and accountability, no 'second instalment' in the drive to attack educational inequality and no new goals formulated for it in relation to the social realities, the new social constituencies and historical tasks of the second half of the twentieth century. Such a programme cannot be detailed here. But some strategic lines of departure can be indicated, from which a renewal of a 'politics of education' from the left could begin. But this will mean — as Bertolt Brecht always insisted — starting not from the 'good old days' but from the 'bad new ones'.

Take 'standards'. Certainly this is a conservative codeword for regressing to the past. It means social discipline, conformity to tradition, respect for authority — the hallmarks of a tamed and subordinated population. Nevertheless, the word is pointing at something real, not imaginary. The left ran away from the standards debate (or made a present of it to the other side, as in James Callaghan's and Shirley Williams's Great Debate), when we should have stood and fought. Of course a comprehensive literacy — and the deepening and enrichment of literacy as a so-called 'life-skill' — *must* be a socialist goal. When did you last see a working person who profited from being ignorant? Of course, the inability of young working people to read and write with fluency and pleasure in a variety of languages is a profound loss to the working class, and thus to any national culture not predicated on privilege. Of course, the failures of some schools either to carry out this primary task successfully, or to enlist the positive support of children, parents and teachers in this historic goal, is a matter for serious concern and collective debate on the left. It is the sign and the site of the permanent subordination — the permanent secondariness — of the working people to those who have 'mastered' (note the gender of the word, for power does not operate in a void) the skills and practices of the advanced literacies of the twentieth century. Ignoring this because the word has come to stand for conformity to their standards, in the authoritarian mode, is not the answer. It is not a mistake they are likely to be making just now at Harrow or Winchester or Roedean.

Take, for example, the prevailing wisdom on the left that

education is really directed at 'self-development' and should therefore have nothing whatsoever to do with the productive system. It is true, of course, that deep damage is done as soon as education is understood as providing 'what industry wants or needs', in the terms that it wants it (docility and discipline) and at the level that it wants it (within the *existing* horizons of skill and attainment). This reductionism — seizing the opportunity provided by recession to impose what otherwise would have had to be done by brute force or dull compulsion — is what is really going on in the youth training and other MSC-inspired programmes. (It is interesting that the state — a Labour-dominated one, please note — had to construct a new apparatus, the Manpower Services Commission, and retire an old one, the Department of Education and Science, in order to fit up education and industry in a desperate tandem.) But it cannot possibly follow from this that a socialist strategy for education, in the context of a structural crisis of the economy which has been going on since the end of the nineteenth century, could really turn on there being 'no connection whatsoever' between education and the economy! The answer is not to fall back on some wholly individualist affirmation of spiritual autonomy, but to go forward to forge a different set of connections. It is how the connections are made, not the fact that they exist, which is the issue.

It is certainly the case that the vocationalist deluge which is now going on, both inside the schools and in the 'further education and training' sectors, is designed specifically to freeze the existing social division of labour between the mental and the manual classes — between conception and execution, as Marx put it — and, within that, to make damn sure nothing much moves on the sexual division of labour and the ethnic division of labour either! But all that does is to reaffirm what we already knew: that education is critical for the maintenance *or the transformation* of the social division of labour. A political force which is determined to do something to begin to break down the expropriation of the people into their separate universes *must* formulate alternative ways of making the link.

The fact is that the very counterposing of 'education' *against* 'vocationalism' and of 'skills' *against* 'education for its own sake' are the only other ways of reinforcing the existing social divisions, because these concepts are already inscribed and imprinted with it. It is the productive system under capitalism which gave education the task of reproducing the divisions in the first place! There are in fact no such things as 'isolable skills', divorced from the general practice of learning in its proper sense, which can be detached and 'taught'. For one thing, if British industry, the MSC or the DES know what skills the working population of the twenty-first century are likely to need, they are certainly keeping it a well-guarded secret. For another, skills which are flexible, adaptable, which can be transformed for the needs and techniques of a century we cannot yet foresee, require two essential ingredients. First, they need to be taught in the context of a general education, what we can call a comprehensive literacy. Second, they should be learned in the context of developing the capacities for their use by the subjects of the process. Everything else is 'keeping them off the streets'. It is not the capacity to turn a lathe like Dad did in 1920, or how to write a letter asking for one of the many non-existent jobs as they used to do 'in the old days'. It is the skills which are basic, *now*, to a class which means to lead, not simply to serve, the modern world. They are the basic, general skills of analysis and conceptualization, of concepts and ideas and principles rather than of specific and outdated 'contents', of abstraction and generalization and categorization, *at whatever level it is possible to teach them*. That is where the teachers − the experts, the professionals − come in: once the general strategic 'political' goals have been set. For the professionals who will identify with this historic task of mass education know something about the variety of pedagogies − and the variety of effects which they have − in relation to particular goals. (There is no general pedagogy: only pedagogies, like horses, for courses.) But the strategic goal − the destruction of the existing division of labour, the termination of educational inequality − is a political, not an educational goal. It has to be set *for*, not just *in*, education.

Take the question of the curriculum. It is certainly true that the curriculum we have inherited is inscribed by a set of cultural and ideological values, which appear as much in its emphases and exclusions as in its content. The problem is that what is often counterposed to it is a policy of 'teach whatever came into your head as you got off the bus this morning' − on the mistaken grounds that there is a sort of 'natural' curriculum, the curriculum of 'life itself', which has only to be exposed to be learned; one which has never been good enough for the ruling classes but is somehow OK for the ruled. There is no such thing. In fact, every curriculum is an ordering of knowledge; every curriculum is constructed through a set of emphases and exclusions and every one is shot through with and predicated on certain values. The question is, *which* values? *What* emphases? *Whose* exclusions? There is no escape into nature from the tough and difficult business of designing a curriculum for a specific set of social purposes. There is nothing simple about the disciplines which are required really to know anything, and no easy escape from them. The point is that they shouldn't be preserved simply as an act of homage to the past; in the imperial spirit of 'they're there because they're there.' In that naive act of sentimental traditionalism we consign the children of tomorrow to be taught through values, the ordering and valuing of knowledge, from the past. And then we are surprised they come out at the other end, unconsciously wedded to respectability, traditionalism for its own sake, the values of patriarchalism, racism and imperialism, terrified into reactionary postures by the very thought of the possibility of *change*.

In order to fill the void between a strategic and a technical approach to the 'politics of education' there has arisen a particular kind of educational 'progressivism'. The practices and pedagogies associated with it have proved priceless in certain respects. I can think of at least two lessons learned in that period which we will have to build on. First, the profound awareness it gave that every educational process is a form of social control. It alerted us to the 'hidden curriculum' of educational practice. Second, its honouring of the forms of life and culture, the languages and values, patterns of communication and interaction − in short, the experience − of the learners, of the excluded classes. But there was at least one profound error, and one piece of unconscious bad faith involved in this approach which has provided the radical right with a point of entry, and which, on the other grounds, will have to be deeply reconsidered. The 'bad faith', to put it brutally and polemically, consisted of teachers, who themselves had learned to manipulate, symbolically at least, two worlds, in effect, patronizing kids with the view that all they needed to know was what they had already absorbed through their pores from 'the great university of ordinary life' when they themselves wouldn't be caught dead subscribing (nor would they consign their children) to the

Point is to (a) take this knowledge seriously
(b) dont prowledge it
(c) work through its good side

textbook of the street alone. The error of thinking which underpinned this was that 'experience itself' is alone the great teacher. Relevance in *this* sense is all.

Now, an educational strategy which is out of touch with the lived relations and experiences of its subjects is, of course, one which signifies that in order to learn in the formal mode of schooling, you must first forget who you are, where you came from and what it is like there. A majority of working-class pupils, faced with the choice, have preferred the latter — and consequently, taking the message only too well, have given up on the former.

On the other hand, what, under our present socio-economic system, 'experience' teaches is also how to be subordinate, how to be second- or third-rate, how to have second- or third-class expectations, how to be run by someone else's agenda of life, how to lose. It also 'teaches' ways of resisting that, and of surviving. But we mustn't tell the story with the negatives left out. We have to work with, but also *work on* experience. We need to bring something to bear on experience. We need to be able to deal with it critically. Above all, we need to be able to see round; that is, to understand the principles and invisible structures on which 'experience' rests and which determines its shape, beyond the naked eye. No curriculum 'tells itself'. It has to be *told and learned*. To evade that hard issue — an issue, yes, of local control and discipline for the sake of a wider freedom — is to short-change the people we teach.

Those who mean to run and transform the world, not just maintain the existing order of things, need to know something more: to learn to expropriate the codes and vocabularies of different experiences. To be confined to one's own experience is to know the world one-dimensionally. That way — it is not too far-fetched to say — lie the roots of working-class racism and sexism, also 'taught' us in the great university of life under capitalism. 'They' secrete and monopolize knowledge because they are only too well aware that knowledge is power — real cultural, technical, social, ultimately political power. Otherwise, they would be giving it away at street corners. 'We' need it: we need more of it than they are willing to give. We need it in our terms, for our purposes. We need it to break subordination, the chains of domination. But it will not float down the street asking to be taken. The idea that the best will do for 'them', and the rest will do for 'us' is tantamount to asking to be taken for a ride. That is why education is a struggle — a struggle *for* something *we need* and they have never been willing to give.

The right have temporarily defined the terms and won the struggle because they were willing to engage. For a brief period in the 1960s and 1970s, the involvement of parents with the school was the left's most democratic trump card. The dismantling of this into 'parental choice' and its expropriation by the right is one of their most significant victories. They stole an idea designed to increase popular power in education and transformed it into the idea of an educational supermarket. There is only one way to fight back, and that is to advance into their territory. That means starting with an alternative vision,. principle and strategy. This may be difficult and complex in its details but it must be broad and clear and unmistakable in its political fundamentals. It is nothing more or less than a politics of education, which aims to break and destroy forever all that is entailed in educational inequality; all that is involved in the monopoly of knowledge, its expropriation to privilege through the mechanisms known laughingly as 'greater choice'. Its politics consists of being able to say to the mass of the people why education and learning are important — not just for some but really for all. Why it is important for individual development — but even more for the development of the subordinated classes, for the excluded social categories. Education is one of the principal areas from which the mass of the people are excluded. Thatcherism is a new, more virulent and self-conscious form of exclusion. The promise of a universal education, and the task of constructing a cultural programme to realize something like this in our lifetimes, is a national popular goal of a democratic kind which, by definition, the party of individual competition, self-interest and 'choice' *cannot* make. They believe in the prize going to those who already have educational power; we believe in an education of the capacities of those who are now excluded from that power. Their horizons and expectations have by definition, to be fixed; ours, by definition, have to be open.

In this article I have concentrated on a broad political strategy for education. I make no apologies for neglecting, as a result, the many important educational themes and questions raised by the other articles in this book — although even they could not hope to cover every aspect of this topic. The basic point is that if Thatcherism wins on the *general* politics of inequality and market competition, it will win in education too. Teachers and parents, and those with a general interest in education, will leave the construction of such a radical national-popular politics of education to the experts at their peril.

2. Educational politics: the old and the new

Richard Johnson

How to respond to educational Thatcherism? As the Thatcher government enters its second term, the question is urgent. There is a sense of being comprehensively outmanoeuvred, yet no clear alternative emerges.

It is complicated, I think, because we are trying to grasp a set of political relationships which have at least three sides. I don't mean the new triumvirate of electoral politics — Conservative, Labour and Alliance — but deeper historical configurations. First, there is the main left-of-centre educational tradition of Liberal or Fabian reform of the public educational system, overtly in an egalitarian direction. This tendency isn't restricted to one party: variants can be found in Labour's traditions, in a social-reforming Liberalism and in liberal Conservatism. It is this formation, which was dominant in the 1960s, which is now in deep crisis. This is especially serious for the Labour Party. Its main educational reflexes have been severed.

The new right has done the surgery and in no very gentle way. This, again, is a tendency rather than a party. It is now dominant within Conservatism and has put down real popular roots. Since the distinctive new right's stance is the main object of this book, there's no need to identify it further.

The third tendency is less easily described. It is a form of politics which is coming into existence. It exists in fragments, and, often, in critiques of the main tendencies. It doesn't have a name. It crystallizes mainly in 'new left' criticisms of 'old Marxism' and 'old social democracy' (which includes the SDP). It attempts to develop a socialism which is non-statist and strongly informed by feminism and anti-racism. It knows there is a long haul to construct a popular alternative to new right politics. It knows that existing agencies won't do.

My own politics are very much of this kind. In what follows I want to try to give them more shape, by exploring the three-sided relationship. I want to compare some features of the 'old left' politics of education with educational Thatcherism. Then I want to look at some starting-points for a new politics of education.

In all this the critique of Thatcherism has an especially important place. I don't mean a few well-aimed criticisms or even that kind of angry, horrified polemic ('How could they!?') that comes so easily, and takes up so much energy. Critique means learning from the object criticized, especially from its strengths. This is necessary if you are to match it. It also involves *self*-criticism. I stress this, because, with some conspicuous exceptions, both these elements are still in short supply on 'the left'. This has delayed the 'new left' adaptation which has to come. There is still a tendency to find trivial explanations for right successes and left failures – the media, the Falklands, weak leadership and so forth. There is still a huge gap between the better ideas that are available and everyday left (and especially Labour) practice. There's a huge complacency about underlying beliefs. They have seemed so self-evidently correct in the face of such infamy that we've neglected to rethink them. So we have also failed to present them persausively and explicitly. And paid very heavily for it.

The old politics of education

If you put 'education' on the agenda of a meeting, most people expect a discussion of the defence or the reorganization of public education institutions. People who know about politics (who know, that is, the old politics) will bring along their copy of the latest policy document. The Labour Party is particularly prolific with these. There's a long tradition of them from Tawney's *Secondary Education for All* (1922) to the awful *Learning for Life* (1982), which I am sure had him turning in his grave. These take a particular form. They focus on the organization and terms of access of public education and have something of the character of blueprints. Prepared by responsible experts, they are canvassed among the people, by pamphlet and manifesto.

Policies of this kind may well be needed – although as a matter of fact, the main enemy has done very well without them. Educational

Thatcherism has been chary of blueprints, and offers instead a public commitment to a *general direction of change*. It has what we can call a utopia. It is easy to miss this aspect, to be fooled by those lawyers, stockbrokers and ex-guardsmen who explain the Tory plans to us. Behind their ever-so-practical exteriors lie hopes and aspirations which are often as speculative and certainly as evaluative as our own. Indeed, modern Conservatism (which has drawn on old Conservatism too) is distinguished by its utopian or mythic elements. Think of the myth of the nation united in war, the myth of Churchill replayed in the 'winter of discontent', the myth of a modern fall from the stable moral certainties of 'Victorian values', the overall myth of a free market economy as a realization of individual aspirations.

In the educational utopia, education is a consumer good, acquired and regulated through the market, according to demand in the shape of parental choice. This is a true utopia — even if it seems dystopic to you and me. It has inspired loyalties, cultivated desires and gives direction in the rush and muddle of everyday politics. It is subject, of course, to practical judgements about how far it is possible to go and, consequently, to assessments of the force of opposition. There are also important strategic choices, not necessarily specified in the broad vision. But the broad vision has already shown there's an alternative to liberal or social-democratic solutions, and has been a basis for campaigns. Simple 'truths' have acquired patient elaboration in the mouth of Margaret Thatcher. This 'regional' utopia also compliments the overall goal: to deliver us to a more perfectly capitalist future, free from the supposed inhibitions of the past, especially strong unions and state socialism. This project is conservative only in the profoundest sense — of changing institutions in order to preserve or develop existing social relations. It does involve profound *changes* of practices and beliefs. Back to Victorian values, indeed! Didn't Marx suggest that bourgeois revolutionaries always wear old clothes?

Labour's blueprints have often been utopian in another sense. They have failed to will the means to the stated ends. When expectations have been raised, they have tended to disappoint. This is partly because policies haven't been pursued with vigour when opportunities allowed. But bad faith has deeper causes. The promises of equality of opportunity are actually unrealizable by the strategies which are chosen. Pragmatic Labour elements often recognize this and back-pedal

like mad. Then the rest of us cry 'cheat!' But the key problem remains evasive. It is important to be explicit about this.

The usual strategy has been to modify the most blatant educational exclusions, especially those that involve obviously different opportunities in separated types of institution. The preferred solution
has been to replace separated institutions with universal provision in
unified ones: comprehensives, tertiary colleges and so on. The trouble is that inequalities have continued to reproduce themselves — now
universally and by less formal means. This is because destinies remain so unequal outside. The social division of occupations, with its
class-, gender-, race-, and age-based hierarchies, define educational
wants and ambitions for most parents and children. Self-betterment
by formal educational means remains a minority strategy because,
objectively, the rewards of certification are few, or, if the level of
certification is less, meagre. There is no magic equilibrium between
hard work at school and college and the distribution of secure and
rewarding jobs. The disjunctions are paid in disappointment,
unemployment and misemployment. 'Equilibrium' costs pain. Those
who respond to this hard truth by preaching education for its own
sake forget that this too requires particular conditions if it is to be
continued or realized in adulthood. How many working-class mothers,
for instance, can find time, energy or a mental independence to spend
time 'on themselves' in this way? So for most people 'opportunities',
in school and after, remain just 'opportunities': slim chances seldom
achieved and often realistically refused.

Some blueprints (I'm afraid that *Learning for Life* is an instance)
make their compromises with this reality, but continue to use
egalitarian rhetoric as pretentious blather. Those that compromise less,
and maintain serious commitments to equalization, actually depend
on *further* conditions. The most important of these is some real
modification in the pattern of adult destinies. It is now doubtful if
this can be achieved by social policy — that is, by cushioning some
of capital's worst effects by state-administered benefits and controls.
(Some of these may still be worth having!) The trouble is that the
cushions acquire a hardness of their own, and turn into sources of
oppression, such as those brilliantly explored in Alan Bleasdale's *Boys
from the Blackstuff* plays on television. This is another set of contradictions in social-democratic solutions which Thatcherism exploits:

social security, or the council housing office, or the electricity board as the immediate sources of oppressions. Is this what old socialists meant when they talked about changing society? I hardly think so.

Of course, the old politics of education did appeal to some social groups. It promised the extension of benefits or a lessening of risks to those already well-placed to compete. The anger at the arbitrariness of the 11-plus exam was especially strong among those who had benefited from education themselves and expected the same for their children. A minority of working-class boys and girls also learnt to work the systems. But the post-war educational reforms have been a source of disillusionment, too — especially those of the 1960s which were promoted with such high claims. They led people to expect palpable benefits from formal schooling when benefits of all kinds were soon to be in short supply. Although we need to know a lot more about the popular responses, the effect seems to have been to strengthen what's been, I think, the commonest working-class attitude to schooling — a suspicion of anything very elaborate beyond the most familiar skills. Though realistic in the short term, this was also fine raw material on which Thatcherite arguments could bite. If my argument is correct, liberal and social-democratic aspirations played a considerable part in setting up Thatcherite possibilities. 'Realism' and 'utopianism' (bad sense) were two sides of the same coin.

The old politics were narrow and unpopular in other ways, too. By focusing on access, they implied that exclusion was the only problem. Of course, exclusions have been real and important parts of the motivation of working-class demands and feminist campaigns. (There are interesting similarities and differences in the class- and gender-based histories of such struggles.) But to focus only on exclusion implies that schooling is quite satisfactory in other ways. The problem is to get it rather than change it. Questions about the nature and organization of knowledge, or about particular curricula selections, or about the ideal results implied by different educational regimes, let alone questions about the control of schooling, are left out of account. Once again these omissions have been supplied by Dr Boyson's promises of 'basics' and parental say.

But the problems are deeper than this. We often by-pass the experiences of that considerable minority who haven't been excluded but have 'succeeded' in education in some measure. Probably this will apply to most readers of this book, and it certainly applies to me. Yet I still find working in education and producing knowledge a deeply contradictory affair, and uncover a lot of pain in the personal histories of students. Of course, this pain is mixed up with real pleasures. Such pleasures aren't necessarily connected with education's rites of passage, those central occasions that give pleasure to proud mums and dads — getting 'A' levels, degrees and so on. Often the greatest pleasures are tangential to the formal business of education — political enthusiasms, friendships, readings which weren't on the syllabus, or emulations of an intellectual but also personal kind. The central occasions always seem more contradictory and disappointing. In any case, there is potentially so much more in the educational universe than getting kids to college or to school.

Utopias — good, bad, ugly

Despite all the talk about being positive, our own utopias are often dusty and backward-looking. The great lack is an affirmative vision of the future, some way out of our present troubles. We need utopias: but what kind?

In British education, the strongest utopian tradition has been tied up with 'progressivism'. There are elements within it that we might steal away and use in new contexts — the idea that education involves activity on the part of the learner, that knowledge is something done, grasped, taken or seized on, and that the best teaching is an incitement to such activity. But progressivism produced bad utopias because it was based on an abstracted conception of human nature and spirited away everything specific to real-life people. When the resulting ideals were tried in the social world, all kinds of unanticipated determinations intervened.

So perhaps utopian thinking should start not from the generalities of 'human nature', but from people's social and historical particularities — from black and white, man or woman, worker, employer and teacher, child and adult and old-age pensioner. Investigate the problems, contradictions and sufferings which attend these conditions and relations in life. Unlike 'old Marxists', attend not only to the direct relations of production, but to the whole range of social relationships. These relations themselves produce wants, needs, lacks; so try to envisage arrangements in which all the related oppressions might be resolved. You start, in other words, in a critique of the present, as it is. Like the best truths of science fiction and fantasy writing, alternatives have a this-worldly quality and are rooted in current circumstances.

In communicating such imaginings, the point is not to provide blueprints, but to incite new wants, raise ambitions and arouse real hope. But we are not just talking about mobilizing visions. Unlike the ugly utopias, good utopias involve further responsibilities. Advertisers constantly address and help to construct our desires, but they are under no obligations (except those which law and professional ethics may prescribe) 'to make our dreams come true'. Like some kinds of politician, they are true pimps or pornographers. They stimulate desires for some special purpose of their own — to sell a commodity, to get into parliament. Our utopias should be different from this in two main ways. They must imagine resolutions on behalf of us all, but especially the subordinated majorities, and they have to be as realizable as we can make them.

There isn't space here to construct an educational utopia of my own, but it may help to be a bit more concrete. Take the case I sketched earlier, the tension between the structure of adult destinies — more technically, the social, sexual and racial divisions of labour — and the aspiration to educational justice. This is one of the deep structural causes of specifically educational oppressions in our society. Since certain kinds of life chances are rationed, formal education has come to perform the function of selection. It also justifies the inequality of outcomes. This has been one of the most important insights of educational theory and research over the past 10 years or so. Formal education is not primarily a source of social mobility or economic growth: it is a source, in the first instance, of the reproduction of relations of inequality and power. This is crude when stated so bluntly, and it certainly isn't all there is to say about education. But it does throw a flood of light upon particulars: upon the centrality of certification in formal education (and its modern extension), upon the tendency to codify knowledge in curricula (so you can pass or fail), and upon the deep structure of individualization in assessment and examination procedures. Above all, perhaps, it explains the centrality of notions of 'merit' or 'ability' in educational ideologies. This is the way major differences of destiny are squared with a humanistic concern for individuals.

Educational conservatives have always made a virtue of these necessities. Their ugly utopias have always involved making the education fit the society. If to preserve the existing order, abilities have to be tied down, minds shackled and skills limited to coping — so be it. The 'generic skills' of today's Youth Training Schemes, with their codifications of pushing, pulling and other infantile acquisitions reveal a macabre contemporary example. Educational Thatcherism, like all educational conservatisms, works back from adult destinies and their gross inequalities, in order to construct appropriate 'educational' regimes. So we have 'hewers of wood' and 'drawers of water' again, except they are now called 'trainees'. But Thatcherism's particular brainwave is to find a further way of justifying the enforced underdevelopment of humans. It cultivates the realism of parents! What better solution than that parents, or those least well placed to compete, should actually 'choose' the educational under-privileging of their children?

Socialists and liberals have most commonly reacted to Conservative dystopias in one of two ways. One response is to accept the division of labour — that managers must manage and workers must work — but refuse to limit schooling according to its logic. This has been accompanied by the tendency to construct childhood as a separate asocial stage: at least schooling guarantees a space in which people can grow! Around this strategy, very typical of Tawney's educational ideas and of some 1960s tendencies, a whole history of frustrations could be written: kids, eager to get on with adulthood even if it didn't seem up to much, refused to 'grow'; realities broke in in the form of economic crisis which made the spaces less easy to justify. Alternatively, some socialists have created utopias in which the problems are solved automatically, that is, by the movement of technology, the forces of production and, following obediently along, the social division of labour itself. Inequalities may not disappear, but at least technology lessens them. The world is full of well-educated workers in white coats. There is no tension between educational ambitions and the needs of the economy because technology and 'growth' are making whizz-kids of us all. So ambitious head teachers can buy in their computers and broaden their curricula in the sure expectation that there will be plenty of new and 'up-skilled' jobs for their protégés. This way of thinking, which seems so odd today, was nonetheless very typical of educationalists in the 1960s and was an important component in the politics of Wilsonism.

In fact it flies in the face of some of the characteristic evolutions of modern capitalist economies. The adoption of new technologies tends not to create jobs but to destroy them, by expelling 'live labour'. It also produces, less an overall increase of 'skill', more a polarization between those who control, design and manipulate other people's working situations and those who lose what control they had over their own labour process. 'Skill' is a notoriously slippery term: it is best thought of, perhaps, as effective control over your own labour which permits the development of a wide range of capacities. In this sense, a major contemporary trend is towards the *de*skilling of work. Fitting education to work, in this context, means deskilling education too!

Skill'

The third possibility is to change the work to permit the development of capacities. This involves subjecting jobs to an educational critique. Most jobs would prove lacking — and to a greater degree than do schools in industrialists' complaints. It is not merely that the required movements, of mind and body, are often trivial and repetitive (though they are), but that people are robbed of skills of co-ordinating and planning their own labour, and, indeed, deciding what to produce. On the other side of the divide, we have a high and one-sided development of skills of the manipulation of materials and persons in which the criteria are narrowed to profit. Of course, a hard-headed Toryism replies to this that it is 'productivity' that must be the test. But what productivity would you get if you really released human energies!

Educational utopias in the future are going to have to be about education and work, like the old utopias of Morris and Marx. They are going to have to challenge the capitalist premises about 'natural' work divisions that underlie the conservative versions. But it's not just a question of the relation between jobs, no-jobs, and education, as though these were only related externally. It's a question of the educational forms of work and the work-like features of education. It is a question of which human capacities are most important for future development. Nor is it *only* a question of waged work and education.

Involved, too, is the whole domestic sphere and the educational relations and possibilities for educational development.

We have, in other words, to attend to the whole complex of educative sites and institutions. I am aware that this does not take us very far and will be adjudged by some readers as utopian (bad sense). My last lesson (I promise) from Thatcherism is this: *they* looked pretty silly 10 years ago too!

Education as a strategy: really useful knowledge

There are other meanings of 'education' in the history of radical social movements. Education has also been seen as a means to social emancipation. It is through education that socialists and feminists, for instance, have come to know that their everyday unhappinesses aren't the result of personal inadequacies but are common experiences, shared by others, and produced by particular social arrangements. Biographies and autobiographies show how 'conversion' was often accompanied by tremendous explosions of intellectual energy, passionate discussion, omnivorous reading, sleepless nights. Also involved was a brotherhood or sisterhood in learning: new friends, new circles, new meeting places. In these moments there has been a kind of liberation of politics too, away from routine, bureaucratic forms and towards a movement-like organization, with a stress on learning and teaching new relationships. It has been recognized that changing the world means changing people's subjectivities, starting with your own. Education has been less an *object* of politics (in the committee room) and more an intrinsic aspect of political struggle itself. People have learned as they've acted and learned in order to act more precisely, more tellingly. Similarly, the main task has been to generalize certain understandings, to win people from their old allegiances, to educate within a whole class or social group. A common mental model for activists at these times has been a religious one, with much talk of conversion, missions and seeing the light. These meanings of education persist in social language today. People still speak of the labour movement and most ward and constituency Labour Parties have someone specially responsible for political education. But like so much of the old left language these terms often sound hollow. Is this because the politics rarely educate and therefore the movement rarely moves?

Such moments of counter-education have been associated with periods of great social disruption, and, very often, extreme political reaction. I first became interested in this history of independent education by learning about it from historians of the early nineteenth century. In this period, popular educational activity, tied in with popular politics, was a way of struggling both against the material changes of the industrial revolution and against the oppressive (and persuasive) activity of a state dominated by propertied social groups. This was the time of the Chartists and Owenites and their counter-educational schemes. But researchers have also shown there was a similar upsurge between the 1880s and the First World War, both among socialists and within the contemporary women's movement. There was a revival of very similar forms: socialist and feminist newspapers, pamphlets, utopian writing, Sunday schools, reading groups and discussion and self-education circles. The socialist revival and the feminist upsurge both occurred in the context of a very reactionary political climate: the 1890s, for example, were perhaps the ideological highpoint of nationalist, imperialist and racist sentiment, soon to crash into the first 'total' war. Counter-education continued on a more limited (but more organized) scale in the 1920s and 1930s, but we probably have to look at the 1940s, and especially at the Second World War, for the most recent period of counter-educational mobilization. I haven't space for a more exact account of these movements. The story of the 1940s (of Forces' education, the discussions of Reconstruction, etc.) has still largely to be written. But it is important to pull out some recurrent features of these episodes. They are important for our utopias as well as for our strategic thinking.

This educational tradition was always about activity rather than 'provision'. The slogan was — do it yourself. This was accompanied, indeed, by an unrelenting critique of provision. There were also distinctive views of educational content, very different from 'shackling minds'. 'Really useful knowledge' began life as a slogan in parodies of the 'useful knowledge' movement, a liberal and middle-class effort to promote the 'diffusion' of economics and science. Useful knowledge was dubbed trivial, irrelevant, or useful only to tyrants. *Really* useful knowledge started out from everyday concerns. It consisted of theories and explanations of why most people were poor (in the midst of plenty), why the state and the law (and the new police) were so oppressive, and why contemporary society shaped character in the way it did — in aggressive, competitive and uncooperative ways. Radicals sought to break down the distinctions between learning and life, between education and work, which they saw coming into being in the new schooling systems. They minimized the distinction between children and adults (didn't adults need to learn too?) and between teachers and taught. They stressed the educative role of parents, friends and neighbours. They refused the distinction between 'liberal' and 'practical' education, or theoretical and applied. Really useful knowledge was both. It was knowledge calculated to make you free, and useful to the knower in that sense. But it required a strenuous effort of reason to throw off thoughtless superstitions and to comprehend the whole range of social phenomena. Moreover, this knowledge had to be generally available: there was considerable impatience with 'conceited scholars' and 'quaint allusions'. Knowledge, like manure, had to be spread around to be productive. If piled up in heaps it bred stink and vermin! Knowledge has also to be pretty polymathic. William Cobbett stressed the importance of learning 'how to do as many useful things as possible'. There was a stress on a general handiness, including the ability to run your own|collective affairs, reappropriating the skills of ghettoized business.

Really useful knowledge involved, then, a range of resources for overcoming daily difficulties. It involved self-respect and self-confidence which came from seeing that your oppressions were systematic and were shared. It included practical skills, but not just those wanted by employers. The list included things like brewing beer and keeping gardens, as well as how to write and how to make political speeches. Really useful knowledge was also a means to overcoming difficulties in the long term and more comprehensively. It taught people what social changes were necessary for real social ameliorations to occur. It also created solidarities and raised levels of literacy and general understanding within the movements. Many radicals stressed its moral benefits, especially how it might win people from self-destructive habits (especially from drink) and make it possible to realize in this world the christian ideals of brotherhood and love.

Strategies today: inside the institutions

I don't believe it is possible or desirable to recreate early-nineteenth-century or even 1940s campaigning knowledge today. Nor do I think it productive to be nostalgic. The point of the historical detour was to show that 'it ain't necessarily so ', that modern conditions too are quite specific. But I do think that we need, more desperately than anything, a 1980s *equivalent* of 'really useful knowledge' which takes account of our modernity, both in its content and its forms. And I'm very committed to that as a project.

One main difference, however, is that the very separations which early-nineteenth-century radicals attacked now have an overwhelming reality, though they are still historical, institutional and conventional — and therefore changeable. I mean the fact that 'education' *is* separated from life in the sense that it occurs in separate institutions. We do think and act 'college' when someone says education, even when we know 'college' is a very specific educational form. Something similar happens with 'politics': we all know (don't we?) that politics is waiting for the next election. As one Conservative MP put it to an angry, youthful Radio One audience, 'You have to sit it out, my dear, you have to sit it out!' Similarly, we all know that 'communicating' or 'entertaining' is what the public media do. These institutions do very powerfully define the practices as such. Yet we all also know, some of the time, that this is an illusion, and by no means a disinterested one. It allows the professional educators, and the professional communicators and the professional politicians to exercise their own forms of power more freely. *They* don't 'sit it out my dear'. Oh no, not they!

All this suggests a dual strategy. We have to *take account* of the institutional separations, but we have also to work to break them down. We can't wish them magically away, as some middle-class socialists try to vaporize their middle-classness, or other comrades go hell-for-leather for 'extra-parliamentary action'. Unless they have established some legitimacy for this rhetoric, they succeed mainly in marginalizing themselves. The same is true of educational strategies. It is necessary to continue to work within the existing institutions despite the contradictions that result. We have to stay in contact, in friction, with the dominant definitions of knowledge, interrogating them for their usefulness. One danger of counter-education traditions is that they become, or remain, parochial, private, sectarian, as tended to happen in the 1920s and 1930s. They may become, in a sense, over-politicized, losing their liberal side or their explanatory ambition. Such knowledges can degenerate into a kind of wish-fulfilment: I declare 'the facts' to be so or so in order to keep up my morale. 'Knowledge' which is whistling in the dark isn't useful in the long term. So we have to keep in contact, indeed be heavily involved, in the activities which mainly define knowledge in our society, for better and for worse.

We have also to recognize, however, that there are ways in which public knowledges in their dominant forms work against the really useful varieties. For succeeders and those who can afford the luxury, knowledge appears mainly for its own sake. It is 'really useless knowledge', valued for its high levels of purity and detachment.Otherwise, 'education' involves a hard competitive scramble for certification mainly at a stage of life when other pleasures are very urgent. It encourages an instrumental attitude to knowledge, as a way of getting on. This, in turn, encourages 'mimicry', the taking on of a 'knowing' style. That is why, in my opinion, the elements of really useful knowledge that *do* exist in schooling occur in the cracks of the system and in spaces won away from, or in tension with, its main pressures. What happens here is an appropriation and transformation of elements of the approved disciplines and curricula, a hard, bitter and very contradictory struggle to produce *critical* knowledge.

It is one of the features of our present situation, different from any other period perhaps, that critical knowledge has been very extensively produced within and around the formal education system. It's going to be important to extend and defend this state of affairs in the coming months and years. The nearest equivalent to really useful knowledge today and of the kinds of networks it requires, is to be found in the radical college-going generations of the post-war decades. But these knowledges (and perhaps these forms of organization, too) bear the marks of their origin in the encounter with the academic forms. They rarely address the popular agenda directly. That is why, though I firmly believe that 'new left' theories will contribute to the new politics, a *second* set of appropriations and transformations is now required.

Outside the institutions: educational politics

There are, perhaps, two major conditions here: popularity and the establishing of a proper political context for educational activity. There is no question of a counter-educational activity of this kind attempting to substitute, on a long-term basis, for the whole system of colleges and schools. Rather, independent educational activity is a necessary basis for the defence and transformation of public education and public knowledges. It's here that, among other things, the new 'policies' will grow. But independent educational forms have to be popular in several rather different senses. They have to be *popularly available* or, to put it in another way, have to overcome or challenge the exclusions of the provided system. These exclusions work in extremely subtle ways through barely visible class and gender-based differences of language, codes, and knowledge. They also work through differences in time available, and differences in access to cultural facilities. Counter-educational forms would have to be posited on these differences and upon different subjective orientations to knowledge (the practical and the theoretical for example) characteristic both of class differences and of the differences between *professional* intellectuals and other teachers and learners. This is much easier said than done. The distance between a certain kind of intellectual refusal and pragmatism and the intellectual's guilty oscillations between talking too much and abrogating any kind of teaching role is well enough known. It is probably in small group meetings that these conflicts stand the best chance of being worked through productively, especially where there is some very specific collective task to be performed. But popularity is also a question of who sets the agenda of enquiry. I have already argued that this agenda must arrive from the everyday concerns or problems of subordinated social groups, though this does not necessarily mean that it has to be a working-class voice, so to say, that 'speaks' them. The corollary of this, however, is that it is practical amelioration and not knowledge of social conditions for its own sake that must be in charge. So the production of 'first accounts' of the experiences of dominated social groups is of prime importance, but these must be developed and worked up in the light of wider-ranging and more public knowledges. Similarly, the critical (but still academic) knowledges must be hailed with the popular agenda in mind.

Of course, critical knowledges which already start from a popular agenda are a privileged resource here, but even these are rarely in a form that makes them popularly available.

Ultimately, such activities must have an explicitly political context. But it is equally important to say that politics must become a lot more educational too — hence the double meaning of my title. We need an infusion of educational activity, including small-group research, right at the heart of our political practice. Research and the wider discussion of its results ought to be part and parcel, for example, of every local Labour Party. The practice of researching local issues would be one means of breaking down the specifically cultural divisions I have described (and I'm sure many I haven't). The practice of discussing results within the party would aid in the production of activists. And, finally, in seeking publication for such findings and recommendations, local parties would be necessarily drawn into the politics of local and national media, rather than merely complaining of biases.

Of course, I know only too well the distance that separates the usual political routines from this kind of model. But the crisis on the left in Britain must force some fundamental adaptations. If it doesn't there is really very little hope at all.

Part two

Education under the Tories

Introduction

In 1979 the Conservatives were elected to cut public expenditure, and to restore 'standards' in education and extend parental choice. Inevitably, there was a tension between the two. According to reports by Her Majesty's Inspectorate, inadequate funding has meant a decline in the quality of education in many parts of the country. Universities, polytechnics, teacher training colleges — indeed all higher education institutions — have been hit particularly hard financially.

What happened during the period 1979—83 goes beyond a simple reduction in expenditure on education. The whole system is being restructured. In part, this has involved the introduction of the Assisted Places Scheme and moves towards the 'privatization' of education: parents with money can now ensure a better deal for their children. This is what 'parental choice' turns out to mean in practice.

Even more significant in the long run will be the provision of training within existing educational institutions under the aegis of the Manpower Services Commission. By these means control over the curriculum and its content has effectively been wrested from the hands of educationalists. Reflecting the age-old disdain for things technical, many teachers have colluded at their loss of control and turned a blind eye to these events. Schooling is now geared more closely to the control of labour in a period of mass unemployment.

The record charted here is a disastrous one for state education. The prospects are frightening.

3. Margaret Thatcher's disaster: the record

Rick Rogers

In March 1983 in the House of Commons, Margaret Thatcher was asked by Labour MP Andrew Bennett to list the major educational achievements of her government since May 1979. She reeled off seventeen. The four to be most proud of, she said, were that the proportion of children receiving nursery education had gone up, as had the number of young people staying on in full-time education beyond 16 and those entering full-time higher education. Finally, she said, pupil-teacher ratios were at their best-ever level.

As these are the traditional pointers of educational advance, that would seem no mean achievement − if it were true.

A closer look reveals a different story. The Tory record in education has been a disaster. Virtually every aspect of it, 'achievements' included, confirms that we are passing through a period of educational neglect and retrenchment almost unprecedented in modern times.

No one seeking education within the maintained sector has been left untouched by the last 4 years: from the pre-school child to the adult seeking a second chance, from the day-release young worker to the university undergraduate.

By 1990 a full generation of children will have gone through a Thatcherite schooling. For many it will have seemed like 1890, down to such absurd realities as using maths books with pounds, shillings and pence rather than decimal currency, and to writing on slates with chalk because the school's cash for more exercise books had long run out. Such reported incidents give a bizarre taste of what it means to slice 10 per cent off education spending in 4 years. By 1983 £2billion had been taken out of education, 800 schools closed, 38,000 teaching posts gone − 11,000 in a single year.

The decline in levels of school provision over 4 years was publicly plotted by the Her Majesty's Inspectorate (HMI) in a series of reports on the effects of local authority spending policies: too few properly qualified teachers, the abandonment of much remedial work, deteriorating buildings, not enough books or equipment, a restricted and contracting curriculum.

Yet the Conservatives claimed from the start to be basing their education policy on the twin planks of maintaining or improving standards and parental freedom of choice. Immediately on taking office, they repealed Labour's 1976 Education Act which obliged local authorities to bring in comprehensive education. Department of Education and Science (DES) statistics show that between 1979 and 1982 the proportion of children in comprehensive schools rose from 79 to 83 per cent of all children educated in the maintained sector. While the repealing of the 1976 Act has not reversed the comprehensive trend, it has held up the development of a truly non-selective secondary system. (In 1980, the Campaign for Comprehensive Education put the percentage of children in 'real' comprehensives — unhampered by creaming by local grammar or private schools — at only 67 per cent.) One-third of the 104 local education authorities (LEAs) still operate, in part or in whole, some form of selective system. Today, 181 grammar and 407 secondary modern schools remain — 15 per cent of all maintained secondary schools.

But it was the 1980 Education Act which set out the ground rules for Thatcherite education. A new formula for school governing bodies was devised giving, for example, parents and teachers a legal right to representation and schools the right to their own governing body. But no timetable was set for implementation and governors' responsibilities over school affairs were not defined. The new arrangements were a poor response to the recommendations of the 1976 Taylor report. Indeed, surveys have shown that many local authorities were already planning more progressive reforms themselves.

Parents were given a legal right to state a preference (not make a choice) to the local authority for the school they wanted their child to go to. Local tribunals had to be set up to hear parental appeals at an estimated cost of £2million a year. Since, on average, over 90 per cent of parents were already able to get their first choice of school and since in the first year of operation (1982) only 9,000 appeals were heard out of a transfer population of one million children, it seems an expensive charade.

The Act also set up the Assisted Places Scheme to provide government grants to parents wanting to send their children to private schools — in Tory ideology, poor parents with clever children trapped in the state system. The scheme was to have cost over £100million. But opposition, including some from the private sector itself, forced the government to reduce the scheme by half when it began in September 1981. By 1988 the scheme is designed to cater for 30,000 children and to cost £55million a year — about the same as the old direct grant school system abolished by the 1974—79 Labour government. So far £12.6million has gone into switching over 8,500 children into the private sector — 22 per cent below target.

As public funds were being channelled to private schools, the government set out to slash the money for school meals, milk and transport. To curb local authority spending, the 1980 Act took away the obligation to provide a comprehensive meals service. Most authorities have obliged — many setting up cafeteria-style services.

In October 1978, 66 per cent of pupils in England had a school meal. By October 1982, the figure was down to 49 per cent. The net cost of the meals service in England was £566million in 1979; it will have fallen by more than half — to £260million — in 1983.

The fixed cost of a meal went up from 25p in early 1979 to a national average of 50p by 1983. LEAs can charge what they like: the range goes from 35p in inner London and Kirklees to 70p in Bedfordshire. In addition, the proportion of school-meal pupils entitled to free meals rose from 18 per cent in 1979 to 28 per cent in 1982.

The 1980 Act also reflects a genuine achievement for the government. It gave parents a right to much more information about schools and it strengthened the concept of effective parental involvement-issues on which previous governments (Labour and Tory) had been very ambivalent. The second clear achievement also came in 1980, with the introduction of a £9million micro-electronics education programme for schools.

The Conservatives also identified 'popular' educational issues, such as parental rights, the notion of choice (often equated with selection), success defined as exam performance, the quality of teaching, standards, and made them largely their own — irrespective of the effects of their own policies. At no time was there a proper analysis of the validity of such notions — as defined by the Conservative administration — to contemporary education, nor of the evidence on such issues as standards or teacher quality. For example, a 1983 HMI report gave promising, if qualified, approval to teaching standards; research from the National Children's Bureau published in 1982 and 1983 (albeit from evidence in the mid-1970s) revealed no substantial difference between educational performance of pupils in the comprehensive and the grammar/secondary modern sectors.

The only other major piece of legislation was the 1981 Education Act on special educational needs which finally came into operation in April 1983: 10 years after the Warnock committee was set up and 5 since it reported. The Act obliges local authorities to provide for children with special needs — because of physical or mental handicap — in ordinary schools. The concept of special need was widened. But the principle of integration has been undermined because no additional resources have been made available by government for local integration schemes.

The rest of Tory education policy has been largely determined by economic policy or by departments other than the DES. As the government has altered some key relationships in education, the power of the DES has waned significantly. The Treasury, Department of the Environment and the Manpower Services Commission now control the bulk of education policy. They have nurtured a growing division between the academic and vocational and the notions of education and training. One example is the development of vocational schools within schools under the new Technical and Vocational Educational Initiative (TVEI).

Second, the government has claimed to be giving more powers of decision-making to local authorities, such as over school organization, closing schools, and the curriculum. But the growing central control of expenditure has severely limited the decisions that LEAs can take.

In March 1983 Sir Keith Joseph announced the introduction of DES grants for LEAs to be spent on specific areas of education — as directed by the DES — such as technical education, provision for 16- to 19-year-olds, and computer-assisted learning.

Attempts by government to create a national core — and very basic — curriculum have yet to succeed. However, the cuts are already ensuring that some subjects disappear from some schools completely.

Following the Trenaman review of October 1981, the government decided to abolish the Schools Council because it was allegedly too political and teacher-dominated. Its responsibilities for examinations and the curriculum were to be divided between two separate bodies, with members appointed by the government.

Efforts to develop a proper educational programme for 16- to 19-year-olds with adequate financial support for individual students were abandoned and the problem handed over to the Manpower Services Commission, which came up with a quite different sort of solution.

But at least a qualified success was achieved when, after years of negotiations between governments, exam boards and teacher associations, a single exam system at 16-plus, combining GCE and CSE, was grudgingly and imperfectly approved in the middle of 1983.

What to do with exam qualifications was another matter. Two out of every three school leavers could not get a job — hence the rise in young people staying on at school. The dole or a short-term place on an MSC scheme were the only alternatives.

Those other 'achievements' outlined by Margaret Thatcher are equally specious.

In 1979, 37 per cent of 3- and 4-year-olds were in nursery or infant classes. By 1981, the proportion had risen by only 3 per cent. In 1982, it fell back again and the February 1983 White Paper proposed a further drop in provision to 35 per cent by 1984–85.

The Conservatives' commitment to nursery schooling was highlighted late in 1979 when DES lawyers 'discovered' that under the 1944 Act local authorities were obliged to provide schooling for the under-5s to any parents who wanted their children to have it. This followed a decision by Tory-controlled Oxfordshire to axe all its nursery provision in 1982. With unseemly haste, the government added a new clause to its 1980 Education Act. Provision became discretionary again.

Taking into account the overlap of the effects of previous administrations' policies, the Tory achievement in improving the pupil –teacher ratio is unremarkable. In secondary schools, it has remained static at 16.6 since 1980, after being 16.7 in January 1979. In primary schools, which experienced a drop in pupil numbers of 11.3 per cent, the ratio has improved from 23.1 in early 1979 to 22.7 in 1980 to only 22.5 by 1982. Overall, the ratio has gone from 18.9 to 18.5 in the 4 years — a 0.4 improvement compared with one of 1.8 between 1974 and 1979.

Spending cuts have decimated the school capitation allowance, which pays for books, equipment, stationery and other materials. Schools have less to spend and more to pay for as LEAs insist schools pay for such items as phone bills, repairs and transport out of money meant for books and equipment. According to a survey by the Educational Publishers' Council, by 1982 over one-quarter of LEAs were spending 20 per cent less on books and equipment than in 1979; some LEAs were down by over 50 per cent.

School library services have been abolished in several areas, such as Surrey. Public library authorities have suffered a 24 per cent cut in real terms in spending power since 1979. Over 500 libraries have shut, restricted hours, bought or replaced fewer books, introduced or increased charges.

In the HMI report on the effects of LEA spending policies for 1981 (published in April 1982) the library and textbook stock in over half the LEAs was condemned as unsatisfactory. Only five LEAs had satisfactory levels of provision under all the major resource headings of teachers, premises, capitation allowance, in-service training, and non-teaching staff. Subjects needing specialist books and equipment for practical work were 'particularly at risk'.

These HMI reports have also highlighted a key item in the Tory record — Britain no longer has a free education service. Many schools are now able to provide an adequate schooling only through regular and substantial contributions from parents. Says the Inspectorate: 'This trend is leading to marked disparities of provision between schools serving affluent and poor areas.' After only two and a half years of Conservative government it described 'a serious threat to the maintenance of standards and to desirable improvements'.

The universities, where the proportion of working-class entrants has been static for several years, were also savaged. In 1980 the universities' recurrent grant was cut by £100million, which they were to find by charging full economic fees to overseas students. Their numbers slumped — as did places for home students. As the universities contracted — Salford suffered a 44 per cent cut — the Robbins principle of a university place for all who are qualified was finally buried. The polytechnics — temporarily a growth area in higher and further education — were unable to pick up all the pieces as they too started to go under the axe. In 1983, just as the age-range began to bulge for the rest of the decade, the government cut back heavily on future numbers.

Mandatory student grants were regularly increased below the rate of inflation; the number of discretionary grants awarded by LEAs fell dramatically.

A DES survey of adult education provision, published in March 1983, shows that in 3 years enrolments on courses had fallen by 20 per cent (from two million). Nationally, tuition hours dropped by 9 per cent, with wide regional variations — 28 per cent in the North, 21 per cent in Wales, 11 per cent in the Midlands. Only the South held up.

As the quality and extent of provision diminished, the 1944 Education Act — supposedly the foundation of the system — was tested almost to destruction by the courts and DES lawyers. Three LEAs were brought before the courts by parents for allegedly breaking the law on sufficient provision. All got off — or got round the law. The Inspectorate produced four LEAs which they considered in breach of the law, while others were discreetly warned they were close to the edge. DES lawyers puzzled over a new legal definition for providing further education and also discovered (briefly) that new obligation over nursery schooling. Overall, education law was shown to be a paper tiger — too vague and too readily overturned.

But what stamps this period is that the government effectively turned its back on the state education system. It championed selection and the private sector rather than the comprehensive schools where most children get their schooling.

In all this, the two Education Secretaries of the 1979—83 government — Mark Carlisle and, from September 1981, Sir Keith Joseph — remained convinced that neither they nor the government were responsible for the disaster. At the end of 1982, the *Times Educational Supplement* commented:

> Sir Keith Joseph has not tried to give the lead which belongs to his office because he is determined to stand back and maintain a pained detachment, lest anyone should suppose

him to be, in some small way, responsible for the shortcomings which he observes within the education system.

4. You ain't seen nothing yet: the prospects for education

Roger Dale

People's expectations of Tory policy on education doubtless contributed to their 1979 election success. Arguments from Rhodes Boyson had struck a popular chord: education was yet another example of an over generous and insufficiently discriminating welfare state; teachers were answerable to no one and had claimed for themselves the right to decide where and what children would learn. For their part, the parents had to lump it. The Tories offered to restore parental choice and to make schools and teachers more accountable to the nation as well as to parents.

Boyson's rhetoric in 1979 was essentially a strategy for opposition, designed to win the support of disgruntled parents. Delivering the goods proved more difficult: it was all very well, and quite easy, to convince parents that their Jilly's or Johnny's school wasn't doing right by her or him; it was something quite different to come up with a single policy that would, at a stroke, improve the lot of every Jilly and Johnny. Of course, no policy could do that because the system is intended to be competitive and hierarchical and inevitably produces failures as well as successes. The implicit promise to make teachers more accountable for what goes on in schools had proved equally problematic. It's not clear *who* they're to be accountable to — is it Her Majesty's Inspectorate, themselves traditionally appointed by and answerable only to the crown? Or for *what*, as the indecisive policies and outcomes of the Assessment of Performance Unit (APU) demonstrate.

What we saw in that first term in office was, in fact, the initial phase of a long-term project. The Tories have, right from the start, reckoned on perhaps three successive terms in office to achieve their overriding goal: to roll back, and eventually remove, the state as the dominant provider of social, educational and welfare services. Just as the whole monetarist project can be seen as having two distinct if linked components − reducing the money supply by cutting state expenditure, and restoring the hegemony of the market by removing the obstacle of the social democratic welfare state − so we might see the overall education strategy of Thatcherism as being spread over two phases. The first phase, which was nearing completion by the time of the 1983 election, involved four main tactics. The growth of the state provision was checked by means of gross financial cuts. The system was more tightly monitored, through the APU and a more active Inspectorate. It was also redirected into more overtly instrumental and vocational channels − constant exhortation being backed up by selective funding and attempts to cut back, or cut out, the teaching of subjects like sociology. Finally, the Assisted Places Scheme, through which the state provides financial assistance to enable parents of limited means to send children to private schools (as long as they are accepted), provided a fig leaf to cover the Tories' failure to deliver the impossible promise of parental choice. In effect, this represents the first step towards handing over responsibility for providing (though not funding) education to market forces.

Two major obstacles stood in the way of these moves but both were pretty well overcome by the election in June 1983. There had been sectors within the Tory Party which defended the broadly bipartisan approach to state education exemplified by the late Edward Boyle, and which were therefore strongly opposed to the whole idea of privatization. Whatever influence or importance they may have had was swept aside by Margaret Thatcher's post-Falklands domination of the party. Second, both the structure of the education system and the traditionally cautious and defensive approach of the DES tended to slow down educational change. This resistance has been overcome by using the lavishly funded Manpower Services Commission to ginger up and redirect the education service. So far, its greatest influence has been on further education, but now a pilot scheme for extending its influence into schools is under way: the Technical and Vocational Educational Initiative makes large sums of money available to enable LEAs to reinforce a technical and vocational education for 14- to 18-year-olds by means of MSC-approved programmes of study. And given the desire to 'vocationalize' higher education as well, it will not be too surprising to find the MSC intervening in that sector.

I want in this article to look briefly at how the ground cleared in the first term of office might be developed in the next. Much of what follows is based on reading the *Journal of Economic Affairs*, a leading intellectual forum for monetarism. It aims to 'provide a platform for economists dissatisfied with the convention that government is capable of creating solutions to most economic problems', and asks authors to 'provide strong conclusions for policy and to show that what is desirable, though thought impossible, can be made possible'. It may be significant that it has carried more articles on education than on any other single subject.

It seems likely that cuts and monitoring, taken together, will be combined in a new emphasis on efficiency. While there is no reason to expect that we have seen the last of the gross reductions in educational expenditure, it seems likely that future cuts will be aimed at more specific targets. The replacement of student grants by loans must remain high on the list, for example. The dual objectives of this strategy will be more efficient use of educational resources, of all kinds, and their selective redistribution into areas which contribute most to the fulfilment of national industrial and commercial needs.

In the long term, maximum efficiency will, theoretically, be achieved by competition: when all schools have to compete for pupils in order to survive, efficiency is *ipso facto* guaranteed. Until we reach that Golden Age (and we're already well on the way in the post-compulsory sector), some state action will be necessary to bring about greater efficiency. But this state action will be designed to encourage and enhance the operation of market forces in the long term as well as to ensure more bang for a buck in the short term. There are two obvious areas where action of this kind is likely — school closures and teacher accountability. The decline in the number of school-age children, shifting population and the effect of an expanded Assisted Places Scheme will put far more schools at risk of closure on grounds of efficiency; at the same time, the emphasis on efficiency will produce a much harsher attitude towards keeping such schools open. Parents and others who insist on the irreplaceable value of any particular school threatened with closure may be given the opportunity to take it over themselves.

For teachers, efficiency will be based on an extension of the present system of monitoring into something much more like a system of individual, or at least school-by-school, accountability. Here what is at issue is the existence of two of the major alleged obstacles to the hegemony of the free market: the state and the teachers' unions. If action in this area were to be effective, it was first necessary to sever the cosy, symbiotic relationship that existed between the DES and teacher unions — especially the National Union of Teachers — from the 1944 Act until the Great Debate of the late 1970s, when the NUT's national influence began to wane. Since then, with the decline in school population continuing to weaken the position of the teacher unions, their relationship with their employers has moved from being a partnership to being one of master and servant. The employers have sought to be very much more directive about who should teach, what should be taught, and to whom. The recent airing of issues like the dismissal of incompetent teachers and short-term contracts for head teachers has prefigured the kind of initiatives we may expect in the second term. These are likely to focus upon the individual rating and differential reward of teachers, and to erode their conditions of service in the name of efficiency. Under this kind of regime, efficiency is the only criterion for assessing the performance of schools. It assumes that the sole measure of effectiveness is the market; social and educational factors simply do not count.

A major impact of this orientation will be on the content of schooling. The intervention through instrumental and vocational channels is dealt with more fully by other contributors to this volume. Here, I wish to do no more than to signal its contribution to the process of restratification which will accompany moves towards efficiency. Market competition is allegedly necessary for the flowering of excellence as well as the more efficient meeting of the national needs: this, it is claimed, cannot flourish under a system which fails to grasp the nettle of stratification, of the superiority of some and the inferiority of others. So, pending the arrival of a totally market-based education system, any obstructive vestiges of egalitarianism must be expunged from the system. This can be partly achieved through its gradual privatization. But the process must, at least initially, be accompanied by selective funding and encouragement of 'deserving' people and 'relevant' knowledge over 'undeserving' people and 'irrelevant' knowledge.

Let me, finally, consider *how* it is proposed to hand education over to the market — and we should be clear that it is a case of handing over rather than handing *back*. In the *Journal of Economic Affairs*, the favourite proposal is to provide all parents with educational vouchers, cashable at the school of their choice. The premise is that it is both inefficient and restrictive on parental choice to force people with different educational needs and preferences to consume the same amount of education. Schools would thus become more responsive to parents' wishes, as educational funds follow the child to the schools of the family's choice. According to Alan Peacock, one of their oldest supporters, full-blown voucher schemes have four major implications. First, they would turn state schools into 'profit' or at least 'cost' centres. Second, they would make all schools derive the bulk of their income from consumers, who would be free to present vouchers to the schools of their choice. Thus schools at present in the state sector need no longer be owned and operated by centrally financed local authorities. Third, schools would have to expand and contract in response to market forces. And finally, in consequence, they would radically alter the whole structure of local government finance.

Note that it is not proposed to abolish state *funding* for education, but to replace state with private provision. (The vouchers would come from the state, though 'topping up' from parental pockets seems to be considered highly desirable.) Suppliers of schooling would respond to state finance by individually directed demand. The idea that schools should do anything other than meet aggregated individual demand and bow to those with the loudest voice or biggest bank balance appears to be missing from such proposals: we must therefore assume that this is what privatization is intended to bring about.

In the run-up to the June 1983 election, there was much shilly-shallying among the Tories about whether vouchers should or could be implemented. Sir Keith Joseph declared himself 'intellectually attracted by the idea'. Lord Beloff, asked to investigate their feasibility, concluded that 'it would be too disruptive' — and was roundly denounced by the *Journal of Economic Affairs*. Sir Geoffrey Howe felt that 'it would benefit those who already pay for their children's education.'

Moves to privatize educational provision are probably more advanced than those for any other area of the welfare state. This is in part because of its scope — education doesn't affect as many people as the health service, for example — and also because unequal treatment is more easily justified in education than in other areas. This is where populism comes back in. From one angle, privatization through some form of voucher scheme could be a vehicle for implementing the 'parental choice' slogan. But if we probe beneath that slogan, it becomes apparent that 'parental choice' would be exercised only by sufficiently wealthy parents and for appropriately concerned parents. And, to complete the circle, that expression of concern would be an index of parents' moral deservingness to receive any superior offerings, to benefit from unequal treatment. Parental choice and parental concern, then, may be seen as mechanisms for justifying the unequal treatment that would result from privatization. The people who morally deserve — or, of course, can afford — more, get more.

It has now been decided that there is insufficient popular or political weight behind vouchers to justify their high initial cost or the opposition their introduction would undoubtedly create. However, a degree of 'backdoor privatization' could be achieved through an extension of the existing Assisted Places Scheme (APS). This would be politically less contentious and would avoid the problem that the exercise of free choice in the market might jeopardize 'national needs'. Despite recurrent initiatives over the past century to make the education system more responsive to national economic needs, the curriculum remains dominated by traditional humanist values, in which the most 'relevant' knowledge has never achieved the highest status. The stubborn process of 'academic drift', which leaves science and technology courses under-subscribed and churns out a glut of historians, lawyers and sociologists, is fuelled as much by students' exercise of choice as by self-interested 'old humanist' academics. In short, absolute adherence to the principles of the free market in education could come into conflict with the government's need to manage the national economy. APS, as a state-administered scheme, could mitigate this problem.

An extension of the APS, even quite a modest one, would inevitably do serious damage to state secondary schooling. The creaming-off of a further cohort of 'deserving talent', allied to the problems of the declining school population, would in many areas lead to reduced provision of resources and also to the closure of some existing schools — to say nothing of the poaching of teachers from the public sector by the frequently more remunerative private schools.

What is seldom considered in proposals for voucher schemes are the implications for schools attended by the majority of children whose parents could contribute little or nothing in the way of topping-up. It doesn't take much imagination to guess what they would look like — especially as existing government cuts have provided us with some clear prototypes. They are under-staffed, poorly maintained and have such inadequate resources that they cannot provide an acceptable level of education (as HM Inspectors have widely recognized). At the same time, we are getting a preview of the kind of educational stratification that would follow the institutionalization of parental topping-up, as the more affluent switch their fund-raising efforts from swimming pools to textbooks and essential equipment. Once again, the sins of parental poverty, 'ignorance' or 'indifference' are visited upon their children.

Before 1979, education was used by successive governments in an attempt to engineer an ever more egalitarian society. Now, under Thatcherism, it is being used to create an ever more competitive, self-interested and divided society. The kind of equality pursued by the founders and supporters of comprehensive education, limited though it may have been, is now seen to be neither possible nor desirable. Instead, a burgeoning populism is multiplying differences in 'deservingness', like differences in wealth. This is at the expense of those who get the minimum, or less, because they can afford — or grab — no better.

5. Turning back the clock

Anthony Arblaster

It is widely believed that the British Conservative Party is essentially empirical and pragmatic in its approach to politics — not tied, as the left supposedly is, to any fixed doctrines and dogmas. This image is one to which liberal or moderate Tories are themselves deeply attached. It is one of the chief complaints of moderates such as Sir Ian Gilmour that the Thatcherite brand of Conservatism represents a departure from this pragmatic tradition. It betrays true Conservatism by adopting the 'ideological' and 'dogmatic' style of politics which should properly be the property of the left.

But this exaggerates the difference between the present Tory government and its predecessors — a difference which has not been sufficiently great, it seems, for most moderate Tories even to disown Thatcher, let alone leave the Tory party. What Thatcherism embodies, in fact, is bedrock Conservatism, the fundamental commitments and 'dogmas' which the party *must* defend, if it is to sustain its role as the champion of capitalism, and which, at a time of capitalist crisis, it therefore *has to* defend.

This is the context in which we need to understand Thatcherism's approach to education, to say nothing of such oddities as Sir Keith Joseph's proclaimed 'conversion' to true Conservatism in 1975, after years, he now thinks, of having been a 'socialist' without knowing it. So long as the post-war capitalist boom continued Conservatives were content to go along with such steps in direction of equality of opportunity as the spread of comprehensive schools and the vast expansion of higher education in the mid-1960s. Some of them may even have believed in Harold Wilson's prescription for the rejuvenation of British capitalism: the replacement, or at least the dilution, of the rule of hereditary wealth and privilege by the institution of meritocracy.

They were not necessarily wrong to make these concessions to Labour and egalitarianism. Neither the limited and very gradual inception of comprehensive secondary education, nor the creation of new universities and the polytechnics have significantly altered the structure of power or the class composition of the ruling elite in Britain. The so-called 'public' schools, which Labour has never summoned the courage to assault, continue to provide, in harness with Oxbridge, the surest route to the top of British society. The presence of one or two belligerent plebeians in Margaret Thatcher's government should not be allowed to obscure the fact that in 1979 her cabinet contained as many old Etonians and Oxbridge graduates as had Balfour's Tory cabinet at the opening of the twentieth century. The traditional governing class continues to govern — at least when the Tory Party forms the government.

Thus, from a genuinely socialist or egalitarian point of view Thatcher's excited rhetoric about undoing 'thirty years of socialism' is, at best, a ridiculous exaggeration of education policy since 1945. At worst, it is propaganda of the most dishonest kind.

Nevertheless, the intensifying crisis of British capitalism, within the context of a worldwide capitalist recession, has convinced the Conservatives that the 'luxury' of educational expansion can no longer be afforded. In such straitened circumstances there is a need to spell out priorities. For the Tories, those priorities mean a renewed stress on the class divisions which underlie our educational structures, and on the traditional class-based purposes of education.

Eighteenth-century proponents of liberal political economy objected to charity schools for the poor as a dangerous, as well as misconceived, form of benevolence:

> The Welfare and Felicity therefore of every State and
> Kingdom, require that the Knowledge of the Working Poor
> should be confin'd within the Verge of their Occupations,
> and never extended (as to things visible) beyond what relates
> to their Calling.

This is a view that has persisted among the ruling class to this day, and underlies the policies adopted by the Thatcher government.

Let us look briefly at post-school education. The contraction which has been imposed on this sector of education has little to do with the demographic decline in the number of 18-year-olds over the next decade or so which in any case was not occurring in social classes I and II, from which come nearly two-thirds of all university entrants (see the *Guardian*, 17 May 1983); and it pays no regard to the fact that more and more school leavers are obtaining the 'A' level qualifications which, since the publication of the Robbins report on higher education in 1963, have been accepted as an entitlement to entry into higher education. Universities and polytechnics are already excluding qualified applicants by the arbitrary and unfair device of raising the entry requirement year by year. (The two 'A' levels prescribed by Robbins have long been deemed inadequate in practice as an entry qualification.)

What the government believes is that too many people are getting higher education. Talk about 'excellence' by Joseph and Rhodes Boyson barely conceals their belief that higher education should be reserved for the traditional ruling class and its supporting academic elite. As yet no universities have actually been closed down, despite repeated threats. No university teachers have been sacked. Thatcher's and Joseph's desire for an exemplary purge, preferably of supposedly left-wing social scientists, has been frustrated by the entrenched, privileged standing of the universities as semi-independent institutions. But many smaller departments have disappeared, and the social sciences and arts have been forced by the University Grants Committee to turn away applicants. At the same time, preference is given to economically 'useful' subjects such as engineering, computer studies and business studies. To suppose that higher education will survive a second term of Thatcherism with no more damage than has already been sustained would be seriously to underestimate the counter-revolutionary dynamic of contemporary conservatism as the plans revealed in the *Observer* (15 and 29 May) during the election campaign clearly indicated. To 'waste' degree courses on those destined to remain outside the ruling elite is merely to nourish frustrations and resentments among those who have been educated beyond what their allotted 'station' in life requires. The planned introduction of student loans will act as a suitable social filter by discouraging potential students from poorer backgrounds. It cannot be too strongly emphasized that these policies are not inspired, as many people suppose, by simple economic considerations. Indeed, the government's policy of bribing academics into early retirement is so expensive that it is doubt-ful whether contraction is actually saving any money at all. But that is not the point. The policy is determined by class and ideological considerations.

Exactly the same type of rationale determines the government's approach to secondary education. To pass on to people knowledge and ideas, to stimulate in them thinking which takes them beyond post-school job opportunties is simply to foment unnecessary discontent with the existing social and economic order. What is needed is not so much education as *training*: a vocational preparation for whatever work may be available in the shrunken economy created by Thatcherite economic policies.

However, the existing public education system is not entirely geared to such miserably narrow purposes; also like other services in the public sector it has been 'infiltrated' (the right's application of the language of counter-insurgency to ordinary civil life is only too revealing) by radicals and liberals. To achieve their purpose the Tories are gradually building a parallel structure outside the control of local education authorities, under the auspices of that well-known educational agency, the Manpower Services Commission. Even BBC's *Panorama* was moved to ask whether Sir Keith Joseph intended 'to hive off the non-academic pupils in our schools to an organization more concerned with training them for work than preparing them for life' (see the report in the *Listener*, 3 March 1983). Just as the MSC's youth employment schemes are specifically intended to provide employers with cheap labour by undercutting the age levels won by hard trade union bargaining, so MSC training programmes, beginning at the age of 14, are intended to undercut the (quite modest) standards of general education achieved in comprehensive secondary schools. And of course they help to undermine the comprehensive principle itself.

There are hopeful signs that educationists are beginning to wake up to what is happening. Education Challenge, a conference held in April 1983, issued a statement expressing its concern 'that MSC ini-tiatives may perpetuate and further widen detrimental divisions bet-ween education and training. There is also widespread concern that the quality and status of state education is being undermined and that this could lead to damaging social divisions' (the *Guardian*, 26 April

1983). Unfortunately, there is little reason to suppose that Thatcher, Joseph and Boyson consider either the division between training and education, or the related social divisions referred to by Education Challenge as 'damaging'. From their point of view such divisions are in all likelihood both inevitable and desirable.

At the other end of the spectrum of privilege and subordination, local education authorities under Conservative control have been spending part of their restricted budget on subsidizing the tiny minority of parents who are rich enough to send their children to fee-paying private schools — even though this may be at the expense of such elementary requirements as the provision of books and paper in the schools for which they have *direct* responsibility.

Thus, in the area of education, as in so many others, the advent of Thatcherism has meant the end of the vague, flexible but nevertheless substantial consensus within British politics founded on certain liberal or social democratic values. The key concept used to be equality of opportunity. That is not to say that all education policy was governed by this principle. No system which allows the rich to buy a privileged start in life for their children is consistent with such a principle. Nevertherless, more than lip-service was paid to it. Comprehensive schools were intended to promote it. So were educational priority areas (EPAs). The Robbins principle — that anyone with two 'A' levels was entitled to a university place — also expressed it, in a limited form.

Although Thatcher has occasionally affirmed her belief in equality of opportunity, she has always insisted that 'opportunity means nothing unless it includes the right to be unequal' (speech in New York, 19 September 1975), and believes that 'equality and opportunity cannot exist alongside one another. What is opportunity if your only opportunity is to be equal?' (speech in Eastbourne, 14 February 1981). In other words the idea is given the weakest of all possible interpretations; and government policy has been consistent with that view. The Robbins principle has already been abandoned. The comprehensive school is being undermined. The current Tory watchword is 'excellence', which carries with it the implication that those who, at whatever educational level, and for whatever social or economic reason, do not attain 'excellence' can reasonably be neglected, or relegated to some inferior style of education, or what the MSC chair

David Young refers to as 'a level of education acceptable to employers' (see the *Listener*, 3 March 1983). Not since Margaret Thatcher's vaunted Victorian age has the moulding of education to the demands of the capitalist class been so blatantly aimed and proclaimed. 'Given time,' wrote Paul Flather of the *Times Higher Education Supplement*, 'a second stint at the DES under a re-elected Thatcher government, he [i.e. Joseph] could engineer a revolution that could see many gains of the 1944 Education Act undermined' (*Marxism Today*, October 1982). Education Challenge expressed a similar fear about the impact of continuing cuts in education. To put the clock back by 40 years would certainly be a devastating 'achievement'.

Faced with this philistine and reactionary policy, a crude and debased economic utilitarianism, there is no need for the left to adopt a defensive or apologetic style of response. Certainly, such advances as have been made in education since 1945 have to be defended. It ought to be possible for a wide spectrum of socialists, radicals, moderates and liberals, to agree on that. But it is in the end unlikely that either parents hopeful for their children, or young people themselves will generally accept the miserable substitutes for education now being concocted by the Joseph-Tebbit-MSC alliance or the visible injustice of excluding qualified young people from post-school education.

In the capitalist democracies of the West, capitalism always exists in latent or overt tension with the popular pressures inherent in democracy itself. The present attempt to discount those pressures and convert education into a mere servicing process for capitalism and the ruling elite constitutes a challenge to democracy itself. Either this counter-revolution will be accepted, or else we must move radically and decisively in the direction of an education system which serves first of all the needs of people, not as fodder for industry or employers, but as whole human beings and potentially active and responsible citizens. This means an education which includes the arts, creative activity, and the study of politics and society, not a mere 'training' for particular tasks or occupations. An increasingly authoritarian capitalism, based on an ever more conscious and planned manipulation of the population, or a participatory socialist democracy: 'thanks' to Thatcherism, that is the choice we are being faced with — in education as in every other sphere of life.

6. Access to what? The case for higher education

Roger Harris

Protesting at cuts, Association of University Teachers' posters on the buses proclaim 'Britain needs its universities'. 'What for?' the passer-by might ask. Hospitals, yes — but universities? For better or worse, the AUT overstates its case. We are in no danger of having to answer! For a variety of reasons, numbers in higher education continued to grow amid the otherwise general devastation of Tory Britain. Horror at the current abandonment of the Robbins principle (access to higher education for all who qualify), actually concerns single-figure changes to the percentage of the population who can study for a degree — just under 90 per cent never get within spitting distance. Since 1979 expansion has been greatest in the public sector of higher education. Along with a few 'parvenu' universities scapegoated by the University Grants Committee, it is this sector where the effects will be felt should Robbins be abandoned.

We might well ask 'What does Britain need its universities for?' when the *Times Higher Education Supplement* (1 April 1983) recently devoted its editorial column to some exemplary fudging occasioned by the embarrassing but surely correct assertion by Max (now Lord) Beloff, that universities are essentially non-democratic institutions. They *ought* to be democratic, and the issue needs to be squarely faced.

In terms of access, the original motivation behind the Robbins principle arose from the policies of Keynesian Tories. Crudely the expansion of higher education served to reinforce the British meritocracy by marginally widening the opportunities for upward social mobility. It appealed to a social class group who form part of the natural constituency of the Tory Party. Curtailment of this expansion is a natural corollary of the acceptance of structural mass unemployment, but has hardly yet matched the percentage rise in joblessness.

Indeed, initial government plans for cuts have been set aside, for they would have led to massive, 'politically unacceptable' cuts in first-year student intakes. University intakes remain cut, however, because all further expansion is to be sanctioned by reversing the old Tory argument against expansion — 'more means worse'. Now we *can* have more if it *does* mean worse — the public sector institutions are to absorb as much as they can of the demand from the peaking of the 18-year-old age group over the next few years, but resources will continue to be curtailed. This is the policy of 'tunnelling through the bulge'. Universities have pegged their intakes precisely to ensure that 'standards' are maintained. The public sector, having collaborated in the marginal extension of an essentially restrictive and non-democratic formula (the honours degree), is not well placed to criticize it — especially at a time when cut-price surrogates are under active consideration by the Department of Education and Science and other bodies.

The defence of degree courses in the face of such alternatives look like the defence of 'serious' work — a refusal to allow the less privileged to be fobbed off with a sub-standard education. That argument is valid as long as the present structure of higher education remains unchanged. We should not assume, however, that it will. We need to look at the ways in which that structure has itself defined 'serious' work — the more so considering how far such structural factors influence what is offered to students. Student demand is influential, given the mandatory grant system. However, since a student has only one opportunity to 'consume', it is a demand based on prejudice and received ideas, and not upon experience of alternatives. The factors determining what is on offer, and the regard in which it is held are therefore of the utmost importance.

The Robbins principle has been met, over the last few years, largely by the phenomenon of 'academic drift', whereby public sector tertiary institutions have inexorably 'upgraded' their work. Courses are graded so that resources and rewards to staff increase as the work of the institution approximates to that of a university — without, of course, reaching *parity*! Equally, they are likely to decline if 'serious' work is lost by the institution. Not only teachers, but local education authorities liked this system because the bill for higher-level work went to the Advanced Further Education Pool — a fund to which all

LEAs contribute — and not directly to the ratepayer. All this meant that 'serious' work was automatically defined as that undertaken by universities, and the public sector had strong incentives to ape them just as the old grammar schools aped the private sector. This all but nullified the potentially positive element of local democratic control of public sector higher education by local education authorities. Only the pettifogging restrictions of local authority finance remained as evidence that these institutions were under local control.

In responding to financial restrictions the University Grants Committee and, latterly, the National Advisory Board (for the public sector of higher education) have created a pecking order within and between institutions. The terms of reference for what may be considered 'serious' change to an increasing degree as one descends from the pinnacles of the system. While no one would suggest that anything that went on at Oxford or Cambridge was other than 'serious' or 'excellent', as you descend from these heights two considerations become increasingly important — is the work 'relevant' and do you constitute a 'centre of excellence'? If 'academic drift' had carried institutions towards an 'essentially non-democratic' ideal to start with, these innovations only make matters worse. A centre becomes 'excellent' in direct proportion to the narrowness and technicality of the specialism concerned, and, therefore, to its irrelevance to undergraduate teaching, let alone to any wider educational aims. 'Relevance' is, of course, a code-word for supplying the nation's 'need' for trained labour and marketable technological innovation. That the nation deems itself to have a superfluity of those very assets would seem to be irrelevant. No doubt over-supply of trained personnel will help depress wages still further.

Acceptance of the terms in which the centres of power conduct debates concerning the future of higher education is a barren prospect. Should we risk 'standards' and fight for the access to higher education of a fraction of 1 per cent of the 18 to 21 age-group while the overall proportion gaining entry is unlikely to top 15 per cent? Or should we join with the elitists in the defence of the ivory tower from philistine intrumentalism? It is all too attractive for the left inside the academic establishment, having discredited the former line as 'social democracy', to take the latter position — offered, by the way, in the THES leader as mitigation for leftists eager to rationalize their privileges within non-democratic institutions. Protected by the twin bastions of academic freedom and impenetrable prose, such 'critical consciences of society' would undoubtedly be safe — *in* no danger because they *were* no danger. But they would be no nearer a satisfactory answer to the question the AUT posters might prompt.

The Labour Party's discussion document *Education After 18: Expansion with Change* seeks a radical shift in debate on access, to focus on the failures of the Robbins principle alluded to above. New national organizational structures and statutory rights drastically to expand access to higher education, along with measures to stimulate demand and internal institutional democracy should be political objectives of those on the left concerned with higher education, whichever party is in power. But they, too, are not enough by themselves to overcome the 'essentially non-democratic' nature of higher education. There is a further problem to be faced which appears on the surface to be ideological, but actually concerns the 'mode of production' of knowledge in our society.

'Elitism' in education has been a perennial target for the left. 'Relevance', 'vocationalism' and instrumentalism have all too often been the platform from which this criticism has been voiced. We should ask why the Tories, too, have embraced these notions in their reappraisal of higher education. 'Elitism' is more than mere ideology, and more than a mere excrescence of the class system — even though it looks, superficially, like the exclusivity of public schools and London clubs. It is a feature of the production of knowledge in modern societies. It is for this reason that it needs to be taken far more seriously than simply seeking to abolish the currency of the 'old school tie' and the 'Oxbridge connection'. Of course, one learns which way to pass the port at high table, but even if the capitalist class were expropriated tomorrow, and port outlawed as a bourgeois deviation, the monopoly that class holds on knowledge would perpetuate them in positions of power in society. This is not simply the result of the superficial sociology of class, as the section 'Education and Power' in the Labour Party's discussion document seems to suggest. To talk of the 'cultural capital' of some families — books in the home, good conversation at dinner, etc. — or of confidence and skills, misses the point that it is the *monopolistic production of knowledge* which is the fundamental limitation. Instrumentalism, in the form of demands for 'relevance' and 'vocationalism', perpetuates the essentially non-democratic division between active *producers* and passive, alienated *consumers* of knowledge. It is, moreover, irrelevant to this structural feature of the production of knowledge whether the father of a member of this elite was a stockbroker or a miner.

'Surely,' you might object, 'the domain of knowledge is so vast that a division of labour is essential for the conduct of research.' Indeed it is, but this is to neglect the point that the *critical reception* of research is an equally essential part of the process of the production of knowledge. It is the capacity for the critical appraisal of what 'experts' propose, and not the opportunity to engage in research, whose restriction is fundamentally undemocratic. The current Sizewell enquiry, the Depo-Provera controversy, not to mention the debate concerning the adequacy of monetarist economics, are all cases where crucial issues, which should be the subject of democratic decision, are debated within an extraordinarily restricted and largely like-minded community. Largely like-minded because of the interests they share, generated by the monopolistic system of production of which they are part. Not everyone can know everything, of course — the point is that *most* people know nothing, and many of those who know something acquired their knowledge in the anti-intellectual setting of an instrumental or narrowly academic education.

By this I mean that what they know has been learned not in the context of enquiry, where the status of what is learned is illuminated by the quesions that it raises, but has, rather, been swallowed undigested by considering only the questions that it answers. It might seem 'academic' to raise such a matter in the circumstances of crisis in which we find ourselves, but it is not. Even now the Tories have found it impossible to resist the pressure for access to higher education to continue to expand, and the mass scale of unemployment itself creates further pressures for the expansion of post-school education. But there is little that is progressive or democratic about expanding access to a system that remains 'essentially non-democratic' in character — that would merely be to enhance the power of a particularly effective ideological state apparatus — and no one can doubt its efficacy who has been in the staff common-room of a school, college or university!

The present circumstances, while creating pressures for the

expansion of access to higher education also create the pressures which intensify the 'non-democratic' nature of the education on offer. When money spent on higher education seems to require justification in terms of its immediate pay-off it is easier to gain acceptance for instrumentalist homilies — 'we study the following subjects in order to acquaint students with the light they throw on the following practical questions.' To ask whether the 'knowledge' that is being applied is *really* knowledge seems no more than a distraction to students who accept such a rationale — it does not help them get the answers the examiners require! Where there is little doubt that real knowledge is to be applied, the question whether our knowing how to do this means that it should be done is likely to generate even more impatience — 'we don't need to bother with questions like that. Making moral or political decisions is someone else's job.' Indeed it is — it should be the job of the democratic process. However, for the very reasons we are examining, there is every likelihood that the democratic process will be even *less* well informed than the experts who are taught not to think about what they do. The extension of democracy in higher education is, thus, an essential part of the extension of democracy *per se*, and not merely concerned with the means of access to other markets — of jobs, culture, etc.

Opposition to instrumentalism in education carries with it another danger, which is also intensified by mass unemployment. This is exemplified by the slogan 'education for leisure' (enforced no doubt), which construes the task of post-school education as *entertainment* — albeit at a 'higher level' than bingo. Students are equally relegated to the status of alienated *consumers* by such an approach, whereas the aim of education, if it is to throw off its 'essentially non-democratic' character, should be the promotion of students into the league of *participants*. So, in attacking the distinction between 'pure' and 'applied' knowledge, I am not at all wishing to press the claims of a purely academic education. It is no more difficult to acquire necessary skills in the context of enquiry rather than that of training. Moreover, skills acquired in the former context are more susceptible to generalization and extension to new contexts than those which are acquired in an unreflective instrumental setting. On the other hand, knowledge acquired as a diversion or an entertainment carries with it no obligation to acquire any skills, or any conception of its application — it is not just diverting, it is diversionary. Anti-intellectualism of both varieties, in addition to being anti-democratic, breeds inflexible and maladaptive attitudes. It is not instrumental, in the long run, to those who possess it, that is why those who have *not* had an instrumental education continue to dominate our society. The educational ideology of instrumentalism is, of course, instrumental precisely for those to whose education it does *not* apply, and the same may be said of the ideology of education as a diversion. It helps perpetuate the power derived from the monopoly over the means of production of knowledge — a power which enjoys a considerable autonomy from the parallel power derived from the ownership of the means of material production, because, so long as the former continues, that class will continue to manage what they cease to own.

This is an issue of practical politics, however, not just of an abstract ideological critique. There are a number of objective factors which favour the further imposition of instrumentalist and 'diversionary' ideologies on higher education: the shortage of resources, the need for national economic recovery, anxiety over job prospects, the power of higher education management out for an educational 'fast buck', the boredom of the unemployed. But there is another set of factors, too: the negligible need of modern industry for technically specialized personnel; the bitter experience of Thatcherite policies among the generation which will principally return to continuing education, and the growing force of the demand in society for just this opportunity to resume an education; the continuing high level of demand for courses which are not an obvious 'meal ticket'; and the growth of popular dissatisfaction with decision-making by 'experts'. It is vital that higher education does not sell these people short, and these social forces can be mobilized in political struggle at the ground level, regardless of higher-level institutional politics. The paramount status of the honours degree for the 18—21 undergraduate, which has always foreclosed the question of pedagogy and curriculum in higher education, is now increasingly shaky. The record of higher education — not just under the present government, but since the Robbins report — is ripe for popular reappraisal. The question of what people are to gain access *to* is as vital a political issue as how or who is to gain that access. Public pressure is growing for expansion across the whole range of post-school education. Within this context there is a real possibility that higher education might change, as it expands, to lose its 'essentially non-democratic' character. Anti-intellectualism would be the ideological means for aborting such a development, and anti-intellectualism's modern guises are instrumentalism and education-as-entertainment. In education, perhaps more than any other sphere, the experience of post-war Labour policies should finally teach us that fighting for institutional change without ideological struggle is futile.

7. Education and training: under new masters

Andy Green

Education and training in this country are undergoing what is possibly their most radical transformation since 1945. As is often the case, the traditional institutions of education and training are being changed by pressure from without; by the advent of mass youth unemployment, a circumstance over which the education system has no control, and through the agency of the Manpower Services Commission (MSC), a government Quango accountable only to the Minister of Employment. What is happening to youth training has been well publicized, if not well understood. Its potential effect on school education has been largely missed, perhaps on account of the unlikely quarter from which it originates. Whilst British educationalists have maintained their customary detachment from industry and vocationalism, the MSC have simply marched up on their unprotected flank, hijacked further education, and are now set to infiltrate the school system.

The Conservative government, seeing that it had the pretext (unemployment) and the vehicle (the MSC) for restructuring education and training, has set about its task with clear calculation and cool determination. Following the publication of an MSC document in 1982 calling for a 'New Training Initiative' the government produced its own White Paper in December of that year, setting out the parameters of a new training system for *all* school leavers, and instigating an MSC Task Group to draw up proposals. It is the Task Group report, which came out the following April, that contains the proposals which may determine the future of all post-compulsory education and training, and transform, in its wake, secondary schooling itself.

The report's central proposal is for a £1.1billion Youth Training Scheme (YTS) which will embrace 480,000 16-year-old school leavers in a year-long programme of work experience, training and/or relevant education. The young trainee will receive £25 per week and spend 9 months in work experience and a further 3 months in off-the-job training provided either by the employer 'on site' or by teachers in colleges of further education.

The schemes have two main forms of 'delivery structure'. The MSC's preferred Mode (A) would involve a firm or consortium of firms or, in some cases, a local authority or voluntary organization, acting as 'managing agents' responsible for overseeing all parts of the provision. For this they would receive £1,950 for each trainee, out of which they would pay £1,450 for the trainee's allowance. The government hopes, somewhat optimistically, to secure 300,000 places in industry on this basis. The other Mode (B) would leave the managing role with the MSC, who would approve and pay other agencies, usually colleges of further education,to run schemes. Colleges would receive funds equivalent to 13 weeks of teaching in college for each student, and would be required to place young trainees in work experience for the remaining 9 months of the year. If work experience placements cannot be found, students will be forced to leave the scheme. The MSC has made it plain that it sees the college option (Mode B) as an unwelcome but necessary contingency if industry and local authorities fail, as they almost certainly will, to sponsor enough places for all school leavers.

The aim of the scheme is, according to the Task Group report, to 'develop and maintain a more versatile, readily adaptable, highly motivated and productive workforce'. The report itself says relatively little about the nature of the off-the-job training and virtually nothing about education. The centrepiece of the scheme is the work experience, the same practice which was the subject of so much abuse under the former Youth Opportunities Programme (YOP) (5 deaths and 23 amputations in 1980−1) and which invoked such widespread criticism for its exploitation of youth as cheap labour and as substitutes for waged workers. The new scheme does not promise to eradicate these practices. It is more likely to erode young people's jobs. There is no guarantee that trainees will be additional to normal intake, only the recommendation that firms should operate a 'favourable' trade-off of three jobs for five trainee places. Despite all this the plan has been hailed as a 'watershed' and 'milestone' in education and a 'new deal' for the young unemployed. It has been welcomed by the TUC, the CBI, and the teachers' unions, all of whom were, in fact, party to its formulation. Why, given these manifest drawbacks, has the Labour movement been so uncritical?

The initial consensus behind YTS in the end may prove temporary and illusory. Rank and file union members were not, in general, consulted and the leadership was, in part, hoodwinked by a clever Tweedle-dum, Tweedle-dee act on the part of Norman Tebbit and the MSC. Tebbit's initial proposals (including the £15 allowance and *de facto* youth conscription) were so outrageous that opponents could unite with relief behind the apparently liberal MSC alternative and savour a rather hollow victory over the Employment Minister when his proposals were shelved. There are also real interests and real needs which will predispose many trade unionists to sympathize with the plan. First, it means vast inputs of cash into ailing further education colleges and the chance to prevent redundancies. Second, and fundamental, is the fact that there is now roughly 60 per cent real unemployment amongst school leavers and few alternatives for them apart from MSC schemes. Any challenge to the MSC has to meet their powerful argument that other more appropriate agencies — the LEAs and the DES — have consistently failed to provide for school leavers. Before the advent of YOP, 60 per cent of school leavers in Britain received no further education, compared with 80 per cent in Germany who do. This may have gone largely unnoticed in days of full employment, but today, with apprenticeships fast becoming extinct, and with most 'non-academic' 16- and 17-year-olds out of work, not to have a policy for youth training is politically unthinkable.

The main case for the MSC's training programme is that it has filled a gaping hole in Britain's educational provision. Its main distinction is an extraordinarily fast and comprehensive colonization of a territory left vacant by others. Since it introduced YOP in 1978, the MSC has led the field, set the agendas, dominated the debate and bought out the institutions. The rest have been left licking their wounds or defending the status quo. There is no question about the political effectiveness of the MSC. But what it has created is an apparatus for control and exploitation of vulnerable young people. The 'new deal' it cynically offers to youth includes neither jobs nor education, and its programme of 'skills training' provides a chilling vision of an army of silent, disciplined and obedient worker drones.

The Task Group's report has a gloss of tripartite consensus between the CBI, TUC, and MSC. Beneath its new educational jargon and its exhortation to 'quality training', however, lies a programme not for improving education or training, but for restructuring the labour force according to Tory political imperatives. The scheme can lay no claim to being comprehensive educationally, but will instead be deeply divisive. It is based on the idea that you educate the middle class (those continuing with 'O' and 'A' levels) and train the working class. It is, at root, both profoundly anti-education and anti-training.

The primary aim of the YTS is the social control of unemployed youth and their re-education in new forms of labour discipline. The origins of the programme go back to 1978. It was clear to the then Labour government that growing youth unemployment heralded not only increasing political dissent amongst youth but also a new problem for the training system: how to accustom young people to the discipline of work when the jobs in which young people formerly got their first taste of work have now disappeared. The Holland report, produced at that time, is littered with references to the dangers of 'alienated youth'. Despite the commissioners' judiciously 'colour-blind' approach, it is clear that the 'spectre' that haunted many in the MSC and CBI was that of rioting, and probably black, youth. The programme that was subsequently adopted, the Youth Opportunities Programme, was based on experiments with summer training camps for delinquents in Canada, and had the clear imprint of social control stamped on its proposal. Anyone who doubts this aspect of youth training schemes need only to go into a typical London college of further education. There they would see unemployed and mostly black youth ghettoized in separate, often antiquated buildings, and 'policed' by security systems including guards, pass cards, glass entry tunnels and, in some instances, dogs.

Although YOP was often regarded as little more than an attempt to get young people off the streets and out of trouble, it would be a mistake to see the NTI as control for its own sake. The novelty of YTS as opposed to YOP is that it involves all school leavers, both those in and out of work, and that it is no longer simply a preparation for immediate employment. The proposals are, in fact, a very bold attempt to restructure the whole workforce (not just the unemployed) in line with Tory economic policy. This can be seen most clearly from the plans to restructure the apprenticeship system. The Tories have argued for many years that British industry is 'over-manned', over-paid, and dogged by restrictive practices and over-powerful unions. YTS is designed to counter all this. By closing down all but seven of the Industrial Training Boards which previously allowed trade unions to monitor training, and by incorporating apprenticeships in-to YTS, the MSC is attempting to reduce trade union control over apprenticeships, to limit so-called restrictive craft practices and 'time-serving', and to reduce apprentice wages. Frank Chappell of the Electrical, Electronic, Telecommunication and Plumbing Union (EETPU) has, predictably, been one of the first to accede to this plan, and has agreed to convert all apprenticeships in the EETPU into YTS places: the would-be apprentice will now serve one year as a YTS trainee on a £27 per week allowance, with no guarantee of further training. This will increase the number of first-year trainees but will also mean that the trainee will receive considerably less money than the tradi-tional apprentice, will have fewer rights, and no guarantee of con-tinued training or employment. For those selected to continue, this training will probably last one more year. This represents a con-siderable shortening and 'deskilling' of the apprenticeship.

The strategy towards unemployed youth is to create a low-wage, unskilled youth labour force. Government dogma has long been that young people are unemployed because they are 'unemployable' or because they have 'priced themselves out of the market'. Both asser-tions are wrong. Young people are more qualified and less well paid, relative to adults, than they used to be. DOE figures show average wages for males under 18 as 41 per cent of average adult earnings in 1975 and 39 per cent in 1981. The MSC tends to reinforce this belief by concentrating on the inadequacies of the unemployed, and the YTS allowance of £25 is clearly designed to reduce youth wages generally. In the Young Worker Scheme introduced in 1982 employers paying less than £40 per week to new young recruits received a bonus of £15 a week. And in a *Sunday Times* interview Keith Joseph ex-pressed enthusiasm for unspecified new schemes which would com-pete with cheap labour in Taiwan.

Although YTS has been manifestly inspired by extrinsic political motives, it does nevertheless contain an implicit philosophy. The

MSC's training objectives have always been derived from their analysis of industrial needs, and their sympathetic, although sometimes critical, attention to the demands of employers and the CBI. What employers canvassed by the MSC have consistently identified as lacking in their young recruits is work discipline, adaptability and motivation. In Geoffrey Holland's words, 'Most employers look for a greater willingness and a better attitude toward work from young people.' As the Industrial Research Unit found in its 'A−Z' study, 'Job skills hardly merit consideration in young people's jobs... the "best" and the "worst" young people in their first job differed not so much in operative skills as in attitudes and personal behaviour.'

Since the political appointment of David Young as its head, the commission has come increasingly under the influence of Tory economic policy and is hastening the process of deskilling and rationalization. Its Task Group has designed a programme which aims to cultivate in young people good attitudes, work discipline, and the acceptance of a likely future of low-paid and unskilled work with frequent job changes and intermittent unemployment.

A programme of skills training premised on the necessity for deskilling manual work might appear to be a contradiction in terms, but this is exactly what the new training initiative proposes. The thinking implicit in the YTS can be seen most clearly from the MSC-sponsored *London Into Work Project*, directed by Dr Tina Townsend − this has been the spearhead for imposing government curricula objectives on YOP courses. Townsend selected 1,000 jobs in three London catchment areas which supposedly represented proportionally the jobs available to 16- and 17-year-old school leavers with qualifications of three 'O' levels or less. Among them were office junior, typist, messenger, sales assistant, warehouse assistant, porter, needleworker, and labourer.

From an analysis of the most common skills involved in these, Townsend listed those which were 'transferable' − that is, those which were used in more than half the jobs. Current MSC advice to colleges is that these should be curriculum priorities. The following list of 'transferable skills' should, therefore, give a good indication of the MSC's preferred syllabus.

Under 'reading and writing'	Reading and writing memos, forms, messages and charts.
Under 'basic calculations'	The four rules of number, mental arithmetic, adding, decimals.
Under 'talking and listening'	Conversing with others, asking questions, following instructions, describing.
Under 'practical'	Use of two-way communications system, push, pull, lift, carry, use of fixed-setting controls.

What is remarkable about this sample of jobs and 'transferable skills' is that the jobs are all semi- or unskilled, and the 'skills' are all basic skills as opposed to 'craft skills'. Apart from the apprentice trainee, whose training will in any case be substantially diluted, most London YTS trainees are clearly being prepared for a particular range of jobs in the so-called 'secondary labour market'. This consists of jobs which are unskilled, insecure, and pay low wages, offer little chance of training or promotion, where employer investment is very low, and where labour turnover is consequently very high. The jobs are often found in small, non-unionized workplaces, and contain a high proportion of black and women workers. Of Townsend's sample of jobs, 80 per cent required no entry qualifications, only 11 per cent involved off-the-job training, and 70 per cent were in workplaces of fewer than fifty employees. Only 34 per cent of jobs paid wages above £40 per week.

The problem with this research is not that it misrepresents the employment situation in London, or nationally for that matter, (although it clearly has a London bias in its extreme lack of industrial opportunities). More worrying is that its prescriptions merely accept the situation. Rather than design training programmes which would enhance the job prospects of young people by giving them skills and qualifications (City and Guilds for instance), the MSC is using Townsend's recommendations to justify courses in 'basic skills'. These will merely train young people to do the unskilled jobs for which they are already eligible but cannot get because of competition from mature adult workers. The objective is, to use Townsend's extraordinary 'newspeak' phrase, 'to increase their *horizontal* mobility' — to make them more adaptable within semi- and unskilled jobs.

The result will be to reproduce the existing racial and sexual division of labour and to augment the growing gulf between mental and manual labour. As new micro-technology is introduced, both old and new skills converge upwards, at design and supervisory levels, whilst manual work is progressively deskilled. YTS trainees will be in the vanguard of the new mass of intermittently employed, mobile, unskilled workers. What is more, MSC training programmes offer nothing concrete to offset the disadvantage of female and black workers in the labour market, despite official equal opportunities policy. Despite female unemployment increasing at five times the rate for men during the 1970s, and despite the continuing segregation of women in traditionally female occupations, the MSC offers virtually no positive action schemes for women. The Wider Opportunities for Women scheme is a solitary, limited exception. On the evidence of the Lewisham Women and Employment Project (*Women and Training, Who Said Opportunities?*) training for girls on YOP courses merely reinforces traditional female job aspirations and provides no wider opportunities through training. At the MSC TOPs skills centres, for the over-19s, women still only accounted for 0.3 per cent of trainees in 1979. The situation is analogous for black students. They come to college training courses to find, not second-chance opportunities, but courses which carry no nationally recognized certification of worth. Their future is assured: unemployment or unskilled work.

The notion of 'transferable skills' was first developed in experiments with rats. In the MSC's use, the 'transferable' tag accurately indicates their concern for labour mobility. 'Skills', on the other hand, does not here refer to specific competences acquired through lengthy periods of training, certified by nationally recognized qualifications, and allowing greater control over the work process than unskilled labour. On the contrary, it represents a process of *deskilling*. What is truly transferable in this context are not skills but good attitudes. According to the MSC's widely used instructor's guide: 'One of the main aims of Life Skills training will be to adjust trainees to normal working conditions, giving attention to such matters as time-keeping, discipline and the maintenance of relations with others.' 'Acceptance of authority' and 'ballroom dancing' are included in the suggested curriculum, along with an injunction to instructors to 'instil in the trainee the intrinsic rewards that a job can offer'. Students who fail to perceive the intrinsic rewards of packing, shelf-filling or cleaning evidently lack life skills.

Not all social and life skills (SLS) teachers subscribe to this vision, either intellectually or in their teaching. But the MSC's ideas are increasingly pervasive, especially in conjunction with the YTS's recommended use of the 'profile' certificate, a document largely concerned with the assessment of attitudes. The manipulative approach to the inculcation of particular attitudes is evident not only in the anti-conceptual bias of SLS programmes, but also in the approach to teaching basic technical skills. In the age of the micro-chip and the disembodied worker, we are to have a vocational skills teaching which has all the mechanistic qualities of an educational 'Taylorism'. To Frederick Taylor, the founder of scientific management and the time and motion study, skills are merely mechanical operations in a labour process geared toward profitable production. Just as Taylor broke the production process down into detailed tasks involving minimal skill (thus also reducing the worker's control and keeping labour costs low), so Dr Townsend's 'transferable skills' are taught as interchangeable mechanical operations, divorced from their cultural and craft context. To Townsend, the skills involved in dough-kneading are identical to those in massage work.

However great the eventual impact of this new vocational ideology on the education system, it is still encountering resistance at present. Uneven response and regional disparities are likely to lead to a considerable variation between schemes in practice. The result will probably be a hierarchy of opportunities in YTS. The fortunate, probably white and male, will receive a diluted apprenticeship with a large employer. The unlucky, particularly young women and blacks in de-industrialized inner cities, will be exploited as cheap labour by a small employer. Many trainees will spend a month experiencing work which requires only 2 weeks to learn, and will be frustrated by the absurdly short period of off-the-job training or education. At the end of the year all trainees will face the problem of having no nationally recognized qualifications of any value, no guarantee of further training, and for many still, no work.

Many trade unionists and teachers will agree with this rather bleak picture but argue that anything is better than nothing, and that if

[handwritten margin note: Not the case in my study we work values 'learn by doing' over-ride classroom knowledge.]

colleges and local authorities get involved the schemes will improve. But colleges have been involved on MSC terms for the past 5 years: that time has left them largely mortgaged, financially and ideologically, to the MSC. Meanwhile, the LEAs have exempted themselves from considering alternatives.

The most dangerous and probably the most durable achievement of the MSC has been both to privatize education and bring it under central control, thereby securing its greater subordination to the needs of industry. It is in this sense the true child of the Tory Black Papers and Jim Callaghan's Great Debate. It has taken autonomy from colleges. It may yet prove to be the Trojan horse that carries Tory education ideas deep into schools where other agencies have failed, creating a new tripartite structure. Any further commitment to MSC schemes by colleges and LEAs, even be it in an attempt to transform them, may well hasten this process.

In many colleges threats of redundancy and the absence of alternative provision for youth may make abstention from YTS impossible. However, general opposition to YTS is growing. Several councils and numerous trades councils have expressed their opposition. At least two unions, the National Union of Journalists and the furniture workers' union, have voted against any involvement, and NATFHE has been pledged to reconsider its involvement in Mode (B) schemes. While this growing disaffection will likely fall short of general trade union opposition at national level, there are still advances that can be made, in the short term, at regional levels. In areas like London and Liverpool YTS, in its present form, simply will not work. Industry will neither be prepared to manage sufficient schemes nor to provide enough work experience placements for young trainees on college-based schemes. This will give the LEAs some advantage. As David Blunkett, Labour leader of Sheffield Council, pointed out in the *NATFHE Journal* in November 1982, 'The strength of local authorities ... is much greater ... than supplicants seem to think.'

If LEAs exercised this muscle in their negotiations with the MSC, they might secure YTS money for provision for 16- to 19-year-olds with no strings — they should at least insist on control over its design and implementation. This could do away with compulsory work experience and guarantee longer periods in college for trainees. * See S. Hall

That would be a significant tactical gain. But the real problem point about working with experience.

is a strategic one — the need to design a system of post-school education appropriate to an age of mass unemployment and accessible to
both school leavers and adults. The Labour Party's alternative is the
rather inanely titled document *Learning for Life*. It recommends a
comprehensive version of YTS, with 'O' and 'A' level students doing work experience. The ILEA's Further Education Unit's *Basis for
Choice* model, although educationally far more sophisticated than the
MSC, shares many of its vocational premises. Neither breaks entirely from the myopic vocationalist ideology that you teach students the
skills needed for local jobs — and so, logically, teach them nothing
when those jobs have vanished. It is a tragic folly that many pro-
gressives in education have, in their haste to avoid the elitism and
'irrelevance' of the old academic school curriculum, rushed to support a training policy that not only leaves intact the old elitism of the
'O' and 'A' level for the middle class, but which also confines
working-class youths, in the old divisive and patronizing way, to a
separate form of training, as bereft of opportunities as anything that
went before, and 'relevant' only in the degree to which it rubs their
noses in it.

We have to go beyond this divisive training—education
dichotomy, and do so without either conflating one with the other
or slipping back into the old elitist anti-technology reflex of the 'liberal
arts' tradition inherited from Matthew Arnold. The whole idea of vocational relevance is, especially in an age of deskilling and unemployment, totally inadequate as a criterion for learning. As the influential
liberal American educationalist John Dewey said back in 1915, education should not be about 'adapting workers to the existing industrial
regime'. We should 'strive for a kind of vocational education which
will first alter the existing industrial regime, and ultimately transform
it.'

Something can be learnt from the wealth of experience that has
been built up by progressive teachers working in this field in the teeth
of MSC obstruction and educational philistinism. The hallmark of this
has been a flexibility of method and an attentiveness to the needs of
students as individuals, and as members of a social group which is
rapidly developing a political awareness of its oppression through
unemployment, racism and sexism. Equally the commitment to a style
of active learning of skills through project and group work has proved

successful, where the old instructional and bookish approach may have failed.

What we still lack, however, is a broader rationale for continuing education, and it is here, I believe, that we really have to start again. We might begin, for instance, by setting aside terms like 'training' and 'vocationalism', and simply ask ourselves what young and adult students really want. The first priority here, of course, is jobs. Not work experience without wages and employment rights, but real paid work, with all that this entails in terms of adult status for youth and the potential for collective strength. However, education, as we well know, cannot provide jobs. That is another, related, but separate struggle. In the absence of paid work, youth and adults are returning to education with new and often very clear expectations. These are inevitably quite diverse, but most commonly they come looking for marketable qualifications, or for a chance to use their enforced leisure to acquire the essential literacy and numeracy skills which their schooling, for whatever reason, failed to deliver, or to widen their general education. Many adults have already gone some way in their own independent study and come to college, after redundancy or having won a relative space from domestic responsibilities, with an urgent desire for intellectual development and hoping that college can provide a structured and collective environment for this.

Our education system should incorporate a programme of open access continuing education which would combine general and technical education according to demand. This education need in no way reproduce the divisions behind 'training' and 'education'. In fact, its express object would be to break down the division of labour in capitalist work, whereby conception is divorced from execution, where 'mental' and 'manual' workers belong to different classes, and where, traditionally, practical skills are denigrated as 'non-intellectual', requiring training, not education. An education based on the complementarity of general and technical education would avoid reproducing those class and gender divisions. But to do this education must always be both, and in paying respect to both, transform each.

In practice this would mean an extensive emphasis on general education for all students. This would involve an absolute priority for numeracy and literacy where appropriate, recognizing, as struggling workers from revolutionary Russia to present-day Nicaragua have done, the fundamental liberating value of those skills. It would also include political education, and the conceptual and expressive skills that allow the confident development and articulation of concepts and ideas about society. This would be a far cry from the MSC's social and life skills, with its studied utilitarian ethos, and paranoid flight from concepts and critical analysis. Conceptual thought cannot remain the property of middle-class education: all education should be centrally involved in the development of enquiry and study skills (critical reading, analysis and generalization) and with the expressive skills of writing, argument and negotiation.

The teaching of technical skills can no longer be measured in terms of their likely use in future work. It may have once been the case that schools taught the working class literacy, but only to the point where they could read dials and bibles. However, schools no longer cease to teach English when students have mastered the work-related arts of form-filling and memo-writing. Similarly we must not cease to teach students further practical skills when they can successfully 'push, pull, lift and carry'. Further, it is necessary to create a positive environment where young women can learn the traditionally male craft skills without fear of ridicule and humiliation. For both men and women it is essential that technical education goes beyond operative skills and gives the opportunity for the understanding of the design and planning aspect of modern production, so that young working-class people may consider how these may be used under their own control.

It is only, as Rudolf Bahro says, with such a 'surplus of education ... which cannot possibly be trapped in the existing structures of work and leisure time' that we may pave the way for the transformation of our existing society, and the creation of one that can adequately satisfy and harness the needs and capabilities of all.

8. Women's work, men's work: the great divide

Christine Griffin

Although the divisions between women's work and men's work that permeate British society did not originate in May 1979, the ideological and economic effect of Tory policies has been to reassert and widen them both in the home and in the labour market. (It may be necessary to note, though it should not be, that such differences cannot be attributed to supposedly 'natural' factors. What constitutes women's and men's work is neither immutable nor universal, but varies enormously between different cultures and across historical periods.)

The explicit aim of monetarist economic policies is to reduce inflation by controlling the money supply via limitation of the Public Sector Borrowing Requirement (PSBR). Following the rigid theories of gurus like Hayek and Milton Friedman, Margaret Thatcher's government has tried to control the economy by fiscal restraint rather than expansionist intervention. The effects on British industry have been catastrophic, with the alarming contraction of the labour market since 1979.

Traditional manufacturing industries like mining, shipbuilding, steel production, and the textile and motor industries were the first to be affected as thousands of manual jobs turned into redundancies. The service sector was next to suffer, with the disappearance of jobs in offices, shops, canteens, hospitals and schools. Government spending cuts in the public sector impelled local authorities to reduce their services in line with their budgets.

The Tories were quick to attribute these disastrous events to the 'world recession', rebutting charges that their policies might be in any way to blame. Two weeks before the general election, however, the government was embarrassed by the publication of the draft report of the Commons Treasury and Civil Service Committee, chaired by their own Edward DuCann. The report, quoted in a *Guardian* leader on 26 May 1983, stated that 'under half of the rise in British unemployment may plausibly be ascribed to the world recession.' The government now has official confirmation that its policies have played a significant part in contributing to the current state of Britain's economy.

As the economy moved deeper into recession, so the UK labour market began to contract. The unprecedented increase in unemployment since 1979 has affected certain groups to a disproportionate extent: young people, women, black people, those with few recognized skills or qualifications, and disabled people. As usual, those at the bottom and on the edges of the labour market were the hardest hit. Whilst Tory policies might not have been explicitly intended to undermine girls' and women's position in education and employment, this has certainly been one of their effects in practice.

The Tories have drawn on a particular ideology of family life to reinforce the effects of their economic policies. The sanctity of family life is a theme which runs throughout their contemporary rhetoric. The family is vaunted as *the* sacred unit of moral order and stability for Society, the Nation and the declining Empire. Ever since May 1979, Margaret Thatcher has emphasized her own role as careful housewife and mother, managing the economy and protecting the cultural values of the Nation. This caring image became increasingly less convincing and more contradictory as the 'Iron Lady' began to make her political presence felt. Nevertheless, a cosily idealized image of the nuclear family, based on the monogamous heterosexual couple, with father in full-time employment, mother as full-time housewife, and 2.2 children, is presented as normal and universal. All alternative family forms are seen as deviant or pathological. Since the nuclear family form is most common amongst the white Protestant middle classes, a majority of the population should logically be defined as deviant.

The ideology is enshrined in recently leaked proposals of the Family Policy Group. This Tory Think Tank wanted to find new ways of encouraging children to become 'self-reliant, responsible, capable, enterprising and fulfilled adults', to encourage mothers to stay at home, and to make families 'more responsible' for 'unemployed 16-year-olds and for the anti-social behaviour of their children'. Paradoxically, one-parent families, the bane of the FPG, are forced to be models of self-reliance and enterprise in order to survive on £43.20 a week — the allowance to which a single parent with two children was entitled in addition to rent in February 1983. Equally contradictory is the promotion of individual fulfilment for all, given that women are trapped so firmly within the home by the FPG proposals.

Of course, the Tories have not been the sole architects of this particular ideology, but they have used it to further undermine girls' and women's position in British society. The reassertion of women's 'rightful' place in the home and of traditional gender divisions has been a common Tory theme. One example of this was Francis Pym's controversial statement that married women should move out of the labour market and allow others to take their jobs.

The effects of government economic policies have combined with these ideological shifts to widen existing gender divisions in education, training and employment for young people. Today's female school leavers have an even harder time finding full-time jobs than their male peers. Initiatives designed to encourage young women to move into non-traditional jobs have come under increasing threat. In times of high unemployment, 'jobs for the boys' are presented as the first priority, with the educated white middle classes at the front of the queue.

It is not simply that young women are being pushed to the more exploited margins of the labour market. They are also being prepared with renewed vigour for their primary role as moral guardians of home and family life — with a little help from an understanding husband, of course. Classes in 'parentcraft' now appear on social and life skills courses in schools, colleges and YOP schemes, aiming to fulfil just such a function. Although women's domestic work is supposedly based on 'natural' abilities rather than learned skills, some young women must apparently be *taught* to be 'proper' wives and mothers in the nuclear family mould.

Of course, Labour also has its own particular brand of allegiance to family life and sexual divisions of labour. The romantic image of 'mam' as the stable foundation of white working-class community life still has powerful resonances for sections of the left. Women's continued exclusion from the better-paid, skilled 'men's jobs' stems partly from the activities of male trade unionists and workers over the past 150 years. Their initial aim was to prevent employers from using women and children as cheap unskilled labour in order to under-cut male wages. Exclusion practices persist today in the form of of-ficial union opposition or less formal harassment, as male workers attempt to safeguard 'their' jobs.

Whilst Tory policies have significantly worsened the prospects of female school leavers and widened gender divisions, Labour's record has been far from ideal. When Jim Callaghan's Labour govern-ment introduced the Youth Opportunities Programme as a temporary measure in 1978, the Equal Pay and Sex Discrimination Acts had been in operation for some 3 years. YOP gave Labour an ideal opportuni-ty to demonstrate its commitment to this legislation, to breaking down gender divisions in further education and training provision, and to encouraging young women into a wider range of skilled jobs. Although the Manpower Services Commission is semi-autonomous of govern-ment control, it does have an official policy on providing equal op-portunities through YOP provision. Unfortunately, this has not been reflected in most of the actual schemes.

Although equal numbers of young women and men have moved through YOP, traditional gender divisions remain largely unchalleng-ed. Young women have been concentrated in non-manual areas, such as secretarial work, sales, personal services and catering, as well as sewing. Young men have worked mainly in schemes involving con-struction, gardening, carpentry, electrical and mechanical engineer-ing. Whilst equal numbers of young women and men have gone into work experience schemes (WEEP), proportionally more females have moved through Community Services schemes, and more males through project-based and training schemes with a greater skill component.

Attempts at breaking down traditional gender divisions in YOP have so far been confined to the publications of specially convened MSC groups and research studies, and to the activities of isolated in-dividual YOP supervisors, special project development officers, and trainees — most of them women. Although the new Youth Training Scheme retains the MSC's official equal opportunities policy, so far there has been little indication that the new schemes will be a signifi-cant improvement over YOP in this respect.

Over the past 10 years, groups of young women, teachers, careers advisers, youth workers, and other feminists and socialists working with young people have developed ways of challenging gender divisions and the assumption that a woman's place is always and only in the home. Their experiences suggest that single-sex groups and positive discrimination policies are the most valuable, relevant and effective strategies in this area. Rising unemployment levels and renewed calls for women to return to the home have undermined some of these gains, but the value of the initiatives and support groups will not simply evaporate into thin air. All political parties, as well as those working in the area of young people's education, training and employment, need to think long and hard about the relevance of their work to the female half of the population.

Part three

Terms of debate

Introduction

The publication of the Black Papers in the late 1960s and 1970s herald-ed a new development in Conservative thought. They were opening salvoes in a campaign from the right to regain the intellectual ground previously dominated in education by a liberal – professional consen-sus. The papers challenged many aspects of the prevailing orthodoxy. They attacked the dangers of 'egalitarianism' and the lowering of 'stan-dards', and demanded the return of an elite form of education and the extension of 'parental choice' through a voucher system.

Each publication was given extensive coverage in the press. The left, still preoccupied with the battle for comprehensive schooling and the extension of access to all forms of education, responded either dismissively or with righteous indignation. The tacit assumption still seemed to be that the institutional measures they were proposing would solve the remaining problems in the schools. Questions about pedagogy and the curriculum took second place.

When James Callaghan took over the agenda of the Black Papers in launching the Great Debate in the mid-1970s, no clear and coherent alternative was proposed from the left. Thrown on to the defensive, the weakness of its position was underlined by the general lack of support among parents for the 'progressive' ideas on curriculum and pedagogy which it had perhaps too uncritically espoused.

To a large extent the right had been allowed to define the areas of educational concern, and so to set the terms of the debate. The articles in this section expose the shallowness and partiality of many Conservative polemics — their use of nostrums about 'discipline' and 'standards' as purely rhetorical solutions to complex practical and in-tellectual problems, for example. But the right *did* recognize problems which are the object of real popular concern and grievance. The left cannot afford to dismiss or ignore these. Rethinking the terms of debate, in short, is not an academic luxury nor just a response to the right's ideological offensive. It is part of the process of working out new educational objectives and programmes which are not hidebound by old assumptions and habits of thought. This is what is needed if commonsense ideas about education are to be changed and popular support won for radical policies and practices.

9. It's only natural: rethinking child-centred pedagogy

Valerie Walkerdine

'Fascinating! More power to you!' wrote Rhodes Boyson to the teacher who denounced her libertarian colleagues at William Tyndale School in 1976. 'I believe we can turn the tide.' The Tyndale affair did indeed prove to be a turning point in the politics of education in the 1970s, a vivid opportunity for ideologues like Boyson and their allies in the popular press to orchestrate a backlash against progressive education. The response of radical teachers has, in the main, been defensive: a rush to support a kind of education which does not stifle individual expression. Because the attack from the right has been in terms of standards, discipline, coercion, it has seemed relatively easy to argue for defending what exists.

In mounting that defence, we have sometimes not been critical enough in examining the way the alternatives are set up. If progressivism is the best we've got, then criticizing it can appear to be capitulating to Black Paperdom. My argument is that there are serious problems about many of our taken-for-granted assumptions about radical practices. I shall try to show what they are by stepping outside a simple dichotomous view of, on the one hand, a liberatory pedagogy which frees the individual and, on the other, a repressive one which contains and stifles it. I therefore look at certain assumptions about children and about liberation which underpin a number of approaches, from progressivism to liberal child-centred pedagogy. This is not just a critique of progressivism, let alone an attack on it. What I am concerned with is that set of assumptions which is shared by the considerable range of positions in which the nature of the individual child is unquestioningly taken to be the natural starting-point for thinking about education.

The Plowden report of 1967, for example, which enshrined the child-centred approach to primary education, stated as an axiom on its opening page that 'underlying all educational questions is the nature of the child himself'. It is this seemingly uncontroversial assumption which I want to question. In the Plowden report, the nature of the child is seen as the only sound basis of educational calculations, outside and beyond the trappings of party politics or ideology. Its power resides in its status as incontrovertible fact. Indeed, the defence of progressivism and child-centredness against the right's backlash has used that nature and argued that the other side has got it wrong about children and about learning. Unfortunately this has meant that it has been politically difficult to raise questions about nature which do not appear to collapse back into agreement with traditional pedagogy. It is true that feminism has raised the problem of 'what is natural?' But often, by stressing the role of the social in the construction of masculinity and femininity, it has let 'the natural' in by the back door, precisely because it has been left untheorized, an empty space.

It is now politically imperative that we raise these questions. That-cherism has, in effect, closed off a defensive retreat to earlier positions. That is why I want to take a closer, more critical look at the foundations of modern primary schooling and of the progressive position.

Setting children free

Liberating children through education from the oppressive chains of capitalist social relations seems an admirable aim. One of the things which makes it a plausible strategy is a set of assumptions about child development. The principal agrument is that children are individuals who develop at different rates, who cannot therefore be taught as a class and who have different needs and interests to be fostered. In the view of 'development at its own pace', childhood and proper growth and development are best served by leaving children as alone, free and unencumbered as possible.

Modern classroom practices therefore focus on the individual rather than on the class. The 1978 HMI report on *Primary Education in England* testified to the 'almost universal occurrence of grouping and individual work' which indicated 'the concern that teachers have for individual children'. Now while it is perhaps important to reiterate that I am not wanting to counterpose the individual to the class, it is possible to demonstrate that these practices centred on individualism, rather than revealing a natural individual, actually and positively construct the individual itself and, at the same time, prohibit us from seeing children in any other way.

Why is it important to see children in another way? When the child-centred approach was coming into its own in the period after the First World War, setting children free was seen as a political and a moral imperative. German militarism was taken to be founded in 'discipline' and the 'grotesque tragedy of German subserviency'. If the German education system had been used as an 'instrument to ingrain these notions in the soul of a whole people', then an individualism founded in child-centredness appeared to offer the democratic alternative. An education based on freedom would produce the democratic, free individual — free not only from fascism, but from the threat of any political totalitarianism or extremism. Those arguing for a shift in classroom practice made such points passionately: 'In the name of those who have died for the freedom of Europe, let us go forward to claim for this land of ours that spread of true education which shall be the chief guarantee of the freedom for our children for ever.'

The assumption here was that the individual, freed from coercion, will naturally choose freedom, democracy, right-thinking. Cynically, one might ask what people chose, of their own free will, in the June 1983 election. But 'freedom for our own children for ever' could equally well be a slogan for Thatcherism. Is not choice, one of the central terms in modern educational practice, the very concept at the heart of Margaret Thatcher's free-market philosophy? In her view, too, individual freedom is stifled by the massive ogre of state control, over-mighty unions, or political extremism — of the left, of course. My argument is that in order to understand how individuals chose to vote for a reactionary government of their own free will, and also for us to be able to produce forms of action which will work towards change, requires us to rethink what 'the individual' who makes choices actually is. The modern, bourgeois individual is not a natural being, which can be cultivated in freedom or stifled in regimentation. It is a particular historical product, brought into being by those modern forms of social organization which proclaim it to be natural and normal.

Modern educational ideas about what is natural, in other words, are not self-evident, but are linked to a particular brand of psychological explanation. The psychological theories and practices then become mutually confirming. Let us take one of the most important propositions — that reasoning is a natural process, which children develop in a particular sequence of stages. In relation to this idea, teachers have developed formal and informal techniques for observing children's development, assessing their 'readiness' for particular materials and topics, and for judging whether learning has actually taken place. But as what they are looking for, as well as the whole way of organizing classrooms, is defined by those evidences and theories, their own evidence is either bound to confirm it or be explained by recourse to some other explanation within child-centredness. It would be difficult for a teacher to step outside the very assumptions which made her or his practice possible at all. Again, the point is that what seems to be the starting-point for teaching — the nature of the child — can actually be seen, on the contrary, to be the *outcome* of the techniques and practices which teachers use every day.

The idea of the natural child which is sanctioned in early education by reference to developmental psychology has, in many ways, a comparatively short history. Although many features of the idea can be traced further back, for our purposes perhaps the crucial moment was in the foundation of psychology as a recognized science towards the end of the nineteenth century. It was one of a set of new human sciences established at that time — a time when poverty, disease, crime and insurrection among a population newly contained in towns and cities were understood as a threat to the established order. These sciences made possible new techniques of regulation and control in which the individual was located as the target of a number of forms of administration, of welfare, health and education. These practices attempted to produce normal and not deviant behaviour, personality, development. They incorporated techniques for the establishment of the normal and natural individual, and thus for re-forming, where possible, the abnormal. It is absolutely central to this enterprise that normality is a characteristic located in a natural universal individual. Normality is thus defined as a set of capacities in the body or mind which, because 'natural', are regarded as pre-social. The social is in this view only an addition and is not implicated in forming the body or mind itself.

The idea of natural child development has often been put forward as less reactionary than a conception of the natural which implies fixed and inherited intelligence — the sort of view expressed by Cyril Burt in the Black Papers, for example. Such a distinction has been important, and has allowed some 'progressive' advances in education. But to pose these two views as the only alternative prevents us from questioning the very specification of the natural in all its workings. It does not allow us to explore how these assumptions operate to produce categories of inclusion and exclusion, and thereby to regulate and produce 'normality'.

I want to illustrate this briefly with reference to one such category of exclusion: the feminine. Consider the 'nature of the child himself', which is, according to Plowden, at the heart of the child-centred pedagogy. The child who is allowed to develop at 'his' own pace is enquiring, discovering, inventive and creative, and, at first sight, of no specific gender. Further exploration of the assumed neutrality of the categories, however, reveals that they are indeed gender-specific. The characteristics which are taken to describe children in general fit those used to talk about masculinity, while those describing femininty relate quite clearly to the terms which describe the old traditional ways of teaching: rule-following, rote-learning, passivity.

Let's examine this in more detail. The location of reason as capacities and characteristics of the body and mind which characterized psychology's use of post-Darwinian evolutionary biology, excluded from consideration the body and mind of the woman. Women were, by virtue of their natures, excluded from all kinds of practices, including access to certain forms of education. Nature, of course, fitted women for child-rearing: their soft, passive gentleness 'was no doubt necessary in the sex to which nature was to entrust the repository of the human species.'

Reasoning, educated women became, in these terms, dangerous women — endangering the future of the species by going against their 'natural calling'. It is not, therefore, surprising to learn that some literature about girls' early achievement and education addresses itself to the 'problem of female success'. The real discovery and conceptualization which form the cornerstones of modern pedagogy are contrasted with rule-following and rote-memorizing — passive ways to success which were outlawed for example, as contributing to 'the tragedy of German subserviency'. From this point of view, success in terms of attainment or correct work can be achieved *in the wrong way*. One aspect of 'the problem of female success' is that it turns out to be no 'success' at all! Instead of thinking properly, girls *simply* work hard — if femininity is defined by passivity, good behaviour, rule-following and the other characteristics of the old methods, then the outcome cannot be 'real learning'.

Moreover, policies for enhancing the development of *children* in general have often been based on the idea that the development of girls in particular is a problem — in other words, how to deal with the fact that boys do not perform as well in the early years of school? The Plowden report, for example, came out in favour of children transferring from infant to junior school at the age of 8 because transfer at 7 favours girls: 'At this age girls are superior to boys as judged by objective tests ... early transfer to junior school may be one reason why more boys than girls are found in remedial classes.' It must be a considerable comfort that girls' performance relative to boys has declined by the age of 16!

One of the strategies which has been used to counter this later success by boys is to argue that girls are too passive and should be made more enquiring — a move in support of more rather than less child-centredness. That approach does not get to grips with a more basic problem, which is the exclusion and downgrading of girls' early success on the implicit grounds that it cannot be 'natural'. Indeed, instead of seeing women's passivity as natural, we might rather see it as enforced — giving up a struggle which they cannot win. Reasoning and educated women have not ceased to be dangerous. Boys who behave in active enquiring ways are 'real boys'; girls, although they can and do succeed in this way, are at best 'tomboys' or, at worst, 'aggressive'. Alternatively, their success can be for the wrong reasons, in which case they are not 'really' capable.

I have explored this example in some detail because it illustrates quite sharply not only that 'the natural' is far from being the universal category it claims to be, but also that it provides the practices, techniques, and categories which produce female success as a problem. I am not arguing for a new reworking of child development to include girls. Rather I am suggesting that we must view as a *production*, rather than as an uncovering, those characteristics which define the normal and natural individual.

Liberatory education

These problematic assumptions about the nature of children underpinned the radical educational progressivism of the 1960s and 1970s. Liberation was taken to mean freeing the individual from a tyrannical educational machine, which imposed mystifying ideas and sorted people into oppressive social categories. This process of classification was identified in the practices of selection and grading. Because of this, the classification system inherent in developmentalism was not recognized as such.

For teachers like myself, who were formed in the late 1960s, suddenly child-centredness was the basis of a revolutionary promise. Our job as radical teachers became central to the struggle for liberation, the classroom became the frontline for the development of revolutionary consciousness. In my classroom I imagined there to be no stifling norms, grades or classifications. There were no class lessons, only the pure joy of allowing children to be individuals in their own right. Loving and nurturing children, observing and monitoring their development combined the earth mother and revolutionary guardian. Femininity was encapsulated in the nurturing, masculinity in the form of the consciousness it liberated.

Because of that history I can understand why the teachers at William Tyndale saw themselves as the victims of a conspiracy against liberation. In their account of the dispute they argued, with an undeniable logic, that 'in many ways [we] were seeking to carry through to a logical conclusion many of the ideas that had seemed exciting in the post-Plowden era, while breaking through the contradictions by reaching out to more radical perspectives and methods.' The pedagogy that they wanted to develop encapsulated all the tenets of liberationist teaching at the time — eroding the distinction between work and play, developing human potential, making relationships between teachers and pupils equal rather than authoritarian. Schools and traditional forms of pedagogy were seen as coercive impositions stifling natural development — hence the proliferation of free schools at the time.

The aim of such practices was to help children throw off the chains of capitalist society, to discover their true selves. But that notion of the 'true self' possesses certain characteristics which were assumed to be naturally given, but which are actually historically produced — through pedagogic practices, for example. So the alternative is not between a schooling which represses the 'true self' and the watchful, 'enabling' teacher who nurtures the child to realize its full creative potential. Education acts positively to define and construct that 'nature'.

This idea that the object of teaching should be to set children free was one of the things that provoked hostility among many parents against what the William Tyndale teachers were doing. It was, for example, working-class parents who were, by and large, the most vociferous in objecting to the erosion of the work/play distinction which the teachers felt to be an essential part of the process of liberation. Certainly their children were not as used to the kind of autonomy as the middle-class children of Islington who had been formed by it (for children's liberation had as much impact in radical child-rearing as in radical education). The working-class children were by and large the most disruptive. Their parents, even the most socialist of them, had not been as influenced by the political events and climate of the late 1960s and saw no signs of the 'standards' and 'discipline' which might either have made education an escape route or at least taught them the value of work. In failing to understand and engage with each other, the teachers had little recourse except to fall back on a kind of professionalism and insist that they knew best. At the same time, the parents and local authority could join together in identifying what was going wrong. Because discipline and standards were being presented by the teachers as opposed to freedom and incompatible with natural development, the only position from which the parents could articulate their worries was a conservative one. The teacher who first complained about the progressive methods at Tyndale identified the main failures as disorganization, lack of learning incentives, unhappiness in children, behavioural problems and divisions between home and school. By refusing to address those problems, by ruling them out of court, the radical position left the field open for Boyson's reactionary backlash and for the parents' dismissal of notions of liberation as 'middle class'.

In 1976, the same year as the Tyndale fracas, Neville Bennett's *Teaching Styles and Pupil Progress* was published. It tried to set up ways of measuring the comparative effectiveness of a spectrum of pedagogic styles, ranging from the traditional to the progressive. Most subsequent studies have maintained this rigid and untenable distinction between forms of pedagogy and their effects. In the 1978 HMI report, for example, references to standards, skills and testing sit uneasily alongside ideas about the needs and interests of individual children. This sort of cocktail — adding a conservative measure of standards and a dash of skills from another bottle of psychological theory — provides no real answers.

Equally, though, a rejection of ideas about 'setting children free' does not mean accepting reactionary arguments. Nor am I proposing a return to chalk-and-talk. The mistake is to envisage these as the only two positions on each side of a reactionary/radical seesaw. To get out of the present impasse these old dichotomies have to be rejected, the terms of the debate changed. In the kind of analysis that I am proposing power does not simply reside either with 'the system' to oppress or with the children to be set free. Power is implicated in the very form of theories and practices which constitute and fix the natural-normal and its exclusions.

These are difficult arguments, not least because they call existing common sense into question. I am also aware that I offer no clear blueprint for teachers to follow, nor easy methods for translating these conceptual realignments into the terms of political struggle. But we have to start somewhere, and I have tried to show why we need to rethink the whole field of debate. It is not just a question of shifting the emphasis from the individual to the social. What we need to understand is how that condition which we call individuality is formed within apparatuses of social regulation, including education. For my part, I think we can no longer afford to avoid questioning each and every one of the commonsense assumptions which have provided the building blocks for our current political calculations.

10. The unpleasant fact of inequality: standards, literacy and culture

James Donald and Jim Grealy

Conservatism, declares Roger Scruton, the smartest of the new right philosophers, 'involves the maintenance of a hierarchy, and the attempt to represent the unpleasant fact of inequality as a form of natural order and legitimate bond.' Not a world-shattering revelation, perhaps, but it does help to crystallize a thought. Could it be that the clamorous conservative rhetoric about educational standards and excellence could actually be an attempt to represent the 'unpleasant fact' that schooling produces social differences as the inescapable consequence of Nature's unequal distribution of intelligence and sensibility?

The habit of treating social inequalities as if they were natural differences is clear enough in the old Black Papers. Their main ingredient was a defence of academic excellence, drawn in debased form from the tradition of conservative cultural criticism that runs from Matthew Arnold through T.S.Eliot to F.R.Leavis and *Scrutiny* — it was no coincidence that the original editors were both literary critics. But they 'naturalized' this position by marrying it to assertions by the (now discredited) psychologist Sir Cyril Burt about the genetic inheritability of intelligence. Polemic was thus passed off as common sense, a statement of fact. The 'declining standards' theme was gleefully seized upon by papers like the *Daily Mail*, and given a gloss of nostalgia — memories of elementary school recycled through the imagery of Hovis ads. But it was still unclear what was meant by the notion of standards. Panics about the content of the curriculum, the quality of teaching, political bias, the attitudes and behaviour of young people, the measurable performance of pupils — all these were jumbled indiscriminately together. In a refrain as old as industrialization, fears about the supposed inability of school leavers to read, write and count were attributed to employers. All this led to a statistical pantomime. The Black Paperites would quote figures to show that oh yes, standards had fallen; their opponents would counter with their own figures to prove that oh no, they hadn't.

This was clearly an argument that could run and run. The trouble is that it ignored what is really at stake in the argument. For conservatives, the appeal to standards is a double-barrelled weapon. Explicitly, it is concerned with protecting the values embodied in established forms of curriculum and teaching — the defence of the academic status quo. In effect, this also provides a way of policing which social groups are allowed access to prestigious forms of knowledge and which have reductive instruction imposed upon them.

Take literacy. Since the nineteenth century at least, this has always had two aspects. It refers, first, to the functional ability to read or write — a 'skill' in the MSC sense. But 'being literate' also retains connotations of a literary sensibility, a familiarity with literature and an appreciation of it. The first sense — 'English' as the first two of the three Rs — indicates the imposition of the rules of 'standard English' and therefore, the devaluation of other forms of the language. A sense of being at home with the standard language is a precondition of gaining access to the cultural capital stored in the national literary canon. So the defence of excellence as embodied in English literature and a concern for general levels of performance in the basic skills of literacy together operate a double exclusion for most students.

The unique cultural significance of English as a school subject lies in the way that it defines and imposes a hierarchic evaluation of different forms of language. Although it is less intimately woven into the fabric of the national culture, a similar pattern can be seen in a quite different subject like mathematics — basic skills for the majority, a tool for speculation for the few. And in this case, the exclusions are as much to do with gender as with class — that bizarre distinction between 'hard', 'masculine' subjects like mathematics and the sciences and the 'soft', 'feminine' arts subjects.

A conservative conception of standards does not just impose a scale of values on forms of knowledge within the curriculum. It also discriminates between people. It ascribes value and legitimacy to certain class-based competences and habits of thought. More than that, it passes them off as natural aptitudes, as instances of individual excellence.

Labour educationalists have often shied away from the question of standards. The thinking behind comprehensive schooling, for example, did not really challenge the existing curriculum. Its main aim was to do away with restricted or privileged access. It therefore proposed a 'common school'. But it usually stopped at this institutional level, and failed to establish a curriculum which could create a 'common culture'. Sometimes, as in Harold Wilson's government during the 1960s, it was assumed that a grammar school curriculum could simply be democratized. In Labour thinking, then, there is a conflict between traditionally conceived notions of individual excellence and a social-democratic commitment to egalitarianism. This can produce the sort of fudging evident in Neil Kinnock's recent essay in *Renewal: Labour's Britain in the 1980s*: 'equity serves the cause of excellence whilst the achievement of excellence encourages the extension of equity.' This tries to slide around the problem. It treats 'excellence' as a commodity which is now monopolized by an elite, but which Labour can nationalize and redistribute as a welfare benefit. It ignores the fact that the concept of 'excellence' is, in this context, inherently divisive, another instance of social differences being presented as natural psychological or intellectual differences between individuals. Perhaps more important, it ducks the real force of the conservative challenge — that what is at stake in education is the production and distribution of a society's symbolic values. Schooling at present maintains and reproduces existing values. The question is how (or whether) it can become a site for the production of new, opposing ones. However much Neil Kinnock may want to, you can't have it both ways. The terms of debate as set by conservatives have to be confronted head on.

After the Conservative victory in the 1979 election, the rhetoric around academic excellence seemed to go quiet, silenced by the overriding commitment to reducing welfare expenditure. The dilemma is neatly summarized in a comment by Sir Angus Maude, one of the architects of Thatcherism. According to the *Observer* on 2 January 1983, he remarked that 'It has always been far too expensive to improve the educational standards of working-class children significantly.' In line with this gloomy logic, reports by Her Majesty's Inspectorate have consistently concluded that cuts in provision have led to a decline in the quality of education. The concern with standards was expressed not in any curricular innovation, but in a rush to testing and monitoring — for example, through the Assessment of Performance Unit's surveys of basic subjects like English and maths. These had been set up in the wake of James Callaghan's Great Debate, but their results proved inconsequential and no one seemed to know quite what to do with them.

The arrival of Sir Keith Joseph as Secretary of State for Education has led to renewed attempts to come to grips with the problems of curriculum and pedagogy in a more thoroughgoing way. This has involved a two-pronged strategy: on the one hand, changes in the selection and training of teachers and, on the other, the imposition of a pseudo-traditional curriculum. If Sir Keith gets his way, graduate teachers will have to have degrees in the subjects they intend to teach. These will be limited to things like maths, English, history and science. There will be no room for 'second order' subjects like sociology, psychology and philosophy. (Sir Keith's phobia about the social sciences — a term now banned from the DES — may cause some problems: sociology, for example, is the fastest growing 'A' level subject.) Teacher training will concentrate on techniques for transmitting these bodies of knowledge at the expense of what Roger Scruton calls 'the fraud of "Education Theory" ' — which, he claims, 'ensures that those who most love and understand a given subject are those least likely to teach it in a state school.'

Scruton's implication here is that a commitment to the effective teaching of a specialized area is incompatible with the theoretical study of public education — questions about the purposes of education, how children learn, the social determinants of school performance and so forth. The opposition leads to a curiously anti-intellectual academicism, in which teachers are not supposed to reflect on why or how they are teaching a particular body of knowledge. It hardly seems likely to enhance the general quality of teaching. Sir Keith Joseph's prep school masters may have known their Latin verbs backwards, but that wouldn't guarantee they'd have the wit to survive the bewildering social and intellectual negotiations of the inner-city classroom, let alone turn them to educational advantage.

Nevertheless, the conservative critique of so-called 'second-order' subjects does home in on a potential weakness in the left's characteristic thinking about education. Scruton, talking primarily about universities, objects to courses like the Graduate Certificate in Education, Communications Studies, Industrial Relations and Women's Studies — the last especially seems to get under his skin. What is wrong with them, he argues, is their method of 'throwing together rival disciplines and of creating artificial links with areas of "relevance" and "social concern" ', whereas education should be built around 'certain recognized academic disciplines'. Now, there is no need to accept either Scruton's notion of a free market of 'rival disciplines' nor his implication of a natural order of 'recognized disciplines'. But that does not mean we can just junk the idea of disciplines altogether. Sometimes the left has fallen prey to a latent empiricism, to the idea that the acquisition of knowledge can do without these formal encumbrances. When it has borrowed its principles from the progressive education movement, this has led to the proposition that curriculum and pedagogy should conform to a particular psychological model of child development. Alternatively, when relevance to the experience, needs or interests of the student has been the organizing principle, the assumption sometimes seems to have been that the nature of the topic will produce its own methodology spontaneously in the process of study.

What is missing from both approaches is a sense of the conventional nature of academic disciplines. These are implicit neither in the human mind nor in topics of study. They embody particular codifications for ordering perception, for producing and classifying knowledge and for appropriating the world in thought. These bodies of knowledge, each with its own history of formation, are organized into the hierarchy of the curriculum. This organization of knowledge is specific to a particular epoch in a particular culture. The curriculum, as Raymond Williams argued in *The Long Revolution*, is always a cultural selection, 'a particular set of emphases and omissions'.

This hierarchy of disciplines is not a natural intellectual order, whatever Scruton thinks. The origins of the school curriculum proposed by Keith Joseph lie in the English universities, especially Oxford and Cambridge, in the latter half of the nineteenth century. The story of its formation is a complex one, but one theme in the reorganization of intellectual life at that time was the construction of a unified *national* culture which at the same time differentiated between categories of knowledge and, again, between categories of people. The science of language, for example, was then conceived as philology. This allowed 'standard English' to be fixed as the national language; its monument is the *Oxford English Dictionary*. By establishing this as the norm, a new evaluative element was introduced into linguistic diversity. Forms now defined as 'non-standard' were no longer perceived merely as different, but as deficient.

At the same time, the study of English literature was being formalized into a discipline. This entailed the creation of a new object of study: a body of texts now defined as English Literature. The teacher of English, whether in university or school, therefore takes on the role of policeman of the national culture. 'It is our job,' said Professor Christopher Ricks in the midst of the 'structuralism' row at Cambridge, 'to teach *and uphold* the canon of English literature' (our emphasis). Champions of English as a discipline have always emphasized its moral qualities. For an early enthusiast like Matthew Arnold, it offered a way of refining a philistine bourgeoisie. But Arnold was also the first school inspector (a sensitive and far-sighted one, it should be noted). He therefore proposed the teaching of literature as a way of civilizing the masses. Thus in the *Golden Treasury* put together by Francis Palgrave — another educational civil servant — we find literature suitably selected and doctored for administering to board school children. This literature is presented as an embodiment of the standard language, aesthetic value and a national identity. It denies the idea of culture as a process, as the outcome of a particular type of work or as the product of particular social relations. Embedded and perpetuated in this formation of the national language and the national literature in the nineteenth century were specific relationships of power. They served a totemic function: through them, people came to experience themselves as members of the national culture, or as excluded from it.

Although English is in some ways a special case, it is by no means the only subject spawned by the formation of an English national culture. Geography and history, especially as relayed through the school curriculum, are other obvious examples. Indeed, attempts in schools to shift away from this nationalistic emphasis in history towards a concern with social history and historical method are now running into conflict with Sir Keith Joseph's desire to impose his pseudo-traditional curriculum. 'There is an irony in the way that a government which is deeply committed to ending nationalization in industry should be promoting the nationalization of its history teaching,' reported Martin Walker in the *Guardian* on 21 June 1983. 'For that is the direction in which centrally-directed curricula and the insistence on the British dimension to history are leading.'

Two things emerge from even a cursory examination of how and why the curriculum has taken on its familiar contours. The first is that the form of the disciplines and the relationships between them are neither natural nor self-evident. On the contrary, they represent the outcome of past struggles for cultural authority, for the intellectual, moral and ethical leadership of society. Conservative educational thinkers like Scruton cannot really deal with this historical flux — hence perhaps their hostility to the relativizing tendency of sociology. Instead, they defend the existing academic hierarchy as if it were an expression of human nature or the human spirit ('a form of natural order and legitimate bond', as it were). The reasons that Scruton's 'recognized academic disciplines' and 'first-order subjects' — science and 'the more elusive discipline of the humanities' — have been recognized as first-order reflect extrinsic ideological ends, and often overtly political ones. In that sense, their claims to a place within the curriculum are no different from those of today's 'second-order subjects', which are justified by their proponents in terms of social relevance or intellectual validity. It's simply a question of whether you want the curriculum to embody and reproduce existing cultural relations, or to be a means of changing them.

This leads on to the second point about the curriculum. The topics around which the disciplines are organized were not lying around waiting to be studied. They are defined and constructed as objects of study through the conceptual apparatus specific to the discipline. 'English' does not precede the concepts and critical methods that constitute it as such, any more than 'history' exists independently of historical method. The topic provides an ideological coherence for the discipline: it is not a part of the natural order. So multidisciplinary studies do not imply the denial of disciplines — logically they cannot do so. What they can do at their best is to pose new questions (or pose old questions in new forms) in ways that challenge the habits and routines of the disciplines, and so bring about much needed intellectual advance and curricular change.

Disciplines, then, have a history and construct their objects of study. What is perhaps most important about them, though, what gives them their power to shape our knowledge and our perceptions of the world, are their specific conceptual apparatuses and methodologies. This much seems pretty uncontentious in relation to, say, the natural sciences. But it is interesting how in his defence of 'humane education' Roger Scruton backs off from the idea of method in favour of more mystical formulations. 'The constraint implicit in humane education... involves the discovery of spiritual relationships,' he reverently assures us; 'it is resistant to scientific method and irreducible to it.' He is particularly hostile to attempts to introduce semiotics into literary studies: 'What proudly announces itself as a method always turns out, on examination, to be an elaborate irrelevance. The sciences from which semiotics borrows its vocabulary are not concerned with the critical interpretation of literature, but with something quite different. They describe language as a natural object, obedient to laws which could be formulated and understood even by the man who could not speak the language and who had no knowledge of the human spirit which found expression through it.' Scruton's attack is by now a familiar one in cultural polemic. What seems to be at the bottom of his objections is a resistance to the idea of a shift of emphasis towards a definable intellectual *method* and away from a concern with a naturalistic individual *response* ('critical interpretation', 'knowledge of the human spirit').

This opposition between method and response is crucial to an understanding of how a school subject like English produces cultural and social differences. We have already noted that, at its worst, a functional definition of literacy can imply mechanical instruction in the rules of an administered language. But what of those students — not more than 60 per cent — who take GCE or CSE English? Some CSE syllabuses, often those designed by teachers for their own pupils, do attempt to introduce an extended notion of 'comprehensive literacy', but the field is still clearly organized around GCE 'O' and 'A' level examinations. These are notable in several respects as modes of reproducing the national culture. Their content is based on the university-defined canon of English Literature. Most books on the syllabus are by authors long dead: there is little contemporary writing and almost no texts which are formally innovatory. The obverse of this emphasis on tradition is the absence of any explicit critical method. Students are not asked to study texts in any productive historical context. Nor are they expected to develop any great understanding of the formal mechanisms which structure literary texts. The study of literature is thus divorced from any formal study of language, the material basis for texts.

Instead, what students are expected to develop is a certain kind of response to texts. This is supposedly based on the free play of an individual's sensibility or critical intelligence, the spontaneous emotional play between reader and text. The use of a body of explicit intellectual procedures would interfere with the authenticity of this emotion. Far from being 'immediate', though, this type of response is generally learned through mimicry. Many students, deprived of any conceptual apparatus, rely on sets of 'critical cribs' to pass their examinations. The more successful learn to emulate the urbane mode of writing of the cultivated amateur, apparently unencumbered by any compromising conceptual baggage. In other words, the notion of response on which GCE English teaching is based means that some children are judged to have an innate aesthetic sense which others lack. Sorting out who does or doesn't have this supposed faculty is what the maintenance of 'standards' in English is largely about. Once again, a divisive class-based training is presented as if it were a natural endowment.

It is this production of categories of 'taste' and 'judgement' that the French sociologist Pierre Bourdieu refers to when he talks about the uneven distribution of cultural capital. In the left's thinking about education, there appear to have been two main responses to this phenomenon. The more traditional position has been a guilty defence of high culture. The nature of aesthetic response remains unquestioned: the teacher's job is to rescue it from the contaminations of popular culture — here seen as the manipulative product of a mass entertainment industry denounced for commercialism and for allegedly trivializing pupils' taste. Frequently a nostalgic distinction is drawn between the degenerate quality of contemporary popular culture and the supposedly more rich and authentic folk culture of earlier times. From this point of view what is needed is the democratization of high culture and the liberation of innate critical sensibilities. The function of cultural education consists largely in inoculating students against the influence of 'mass culture'.

The other response has dismissed the national culture as irrelevant, sheer bourgeois mystification. The real educational task, it is argued, is to liberate exploited or oppressed groups (the working class, blacks, women or whoever) by re-presenting their language and culture to them. Members of the oppressed groups are assumed to possess already a progressive or revolutionary culture which is only held in check by the weight of bourgeois culture imposed by the school and the other institutions of civil society. It should therefore be the job of the teacher to facilitate self-expression by the oppressed, not to examine concepts or to develop a child's intellectual faculties. The pedagogy associated with this position characteristically encourages creative writing, autobiographical fictions and poetry at the expense of developing a more distanced, analytical approach to culture.

Both these approaches assume that education should be concerned with the liberation of something innate within the pupil — in this way, they share the conservative emphasis on the nature of response and the expression of human spirit at the expense of critical method. By accepting the given definitions of aesthetics and culture, they affirm and naturalize an absolute distinction between a dominant culture and the subordinate cultures which it governs.

What is needed instead, we would argue, is a set of strategies which could move beyond these positions. Again, literature and cultural studies can stand as an example for broader considerations about the curriculum.

The shift we are suggesting is from the concentration on individual aptitudes and sensibilities to an emphasis on cognitive work and the building of knowledge. This would mean that the study of literature would no longer be a matter of self-cultivation or the mimicry of certain rhetorical modes of speech and writing. Instead students would learn about the material and historical nature of 'cultural objects', about their availability for public examination and analysis, and about the work actually performed in the civil society by such objects. The emphasis of teaching, therefore, would be on how language and culture *work*, not on the nation's cultural heritage as objects of mysterious richness.

This approach also has implications for the teaching of writing.

Analysis should not be divorced from performance. Of course, this does not mean the end of 'literature' in the sense of banishing the study and practice of imaginative writing from the classroom. The exercise of imagination, the transformation in fantasy of experience and desire, the testing of literary forms, the attempt to explore the potentialities of language: these have a crucial place in education. Engagement with symbolic forms is, for any subject, a way of achieving a certain perspective from which to understand the place of self in the social world. This should not be conceived as either the self-expression pursued by much progressive teaching, nor as simply one's initiation rites into membership of a fixed culture, as implied by much traditional teaching. Rather, it should provide a means of understanding the world and of showing that it can be changed.

There is no question of sweeping away the curriculum. The desire for an absolute *tabula rasa*, the infantile notion of liberation from culture argued by a certain part of the left, is simply not an option. Socialists should not shy away from the existence of disciplines. Nor need we fear the hierarchical nature of the curriculum — we too are in the business of creating and ordering new criteria of value, as well as countering the existing order. What is called for is a new clarity about the kind of curriculum we need for the building of a critical socialist democracy. The school curriculum is a crucial area for the construction of a popular national culture and for the moulding of the imaginative relations to it of groups and individuals.

We therefore need to begin by questioning existing divisions in the curriculum. We need to ask about the divisions between academic study and manual training, and the denigration of the latter, in much left writing on education. We should challenge the opposition between science and the humanities — itself a curious relic of the English bourgeoisie's uneasy relationship to aristocratic culture. In this respect we also need to consider the continuation of that emphasis in left intellectual work. The sparseness on the left of writing on science in contrast to the large and ever-increasing amount of work in the area of the humanities is an index of the narrowness of the ground on which socialist intellectuals are currently waging the battle of ideas. Pedagogy and the curriculum should also pay more serious attention to the question of popular culture. It is pointless regretting its centrality in the formation of students' cultural identity, or bringing it in as a condescending sop to their taste. It is notable, both in the school and tertiary curriculum, that the best work in film, media and cultural studies is often not only intellectually more ambitious than conventional English studies, but also attempts to engage with students' own experience and culture in a far more serious way. This work does not seek to 'liberate' those things. On the contrary, it starts by considering unquestioned (but always socially constructed) attitudes and beliefs and submitting them to a critical examination in the attempt to develop a more elaborated and coherent 'common sense'.

All these cases imply that an education concerned primarily with teaching techniques of critical conceptual analysis would always question (not deny) the formation of disciplines within the curriculum. It would not simply accept and transmit the cultural connotations of specialized sets of knowledge, responses or attitudes. The educational strategy we are proposing is one that would emphasize the development of people's intellectual capacities, but not one that would reproduce the present castes and coteries of specialist intellectuals.

As custodians of the idols of their tribe, English intellectuals stand indicted for a baleful lack of cultural imagination. The evidence is the narrowness and often triviality of the curriculum at all levels of education — a witlessness writ large in Keith Joseph's plans to introduce a watered-down version of a nineteenth-century public school syllabus as appropriate to British schools at the end of the twentieth century. Against this curriculum's spurious claims to the legitimacy of tradition, as though it were the expression of enduring academic and intellectual excellence, we need to work towards a curriculum that can sustain an alternative vision. That does not mean starting from scratch, but reworking and developing elements that already exist. Even though now it serves to reproduce inequitable social relations, universal education is a precondition for a genuinely democratic society. The challenge is to contest the divisive outcomes of existing state education and, at the same time, to build upon its democratic possibilities.

That is where standards come in. These are not, as conservatives claim, a natural order, nor neutral criteria for measuring educational performance. (About the only thing that can be measured with any certainty are government expenditure and material provision: on that, although it was a Labour government that began the cuts in the mid-1970s, the Tories have a particularly rotten record.) The question you should always ask is, whose standards? And standards of what?

No one would deny, for example, that there are good, bad and indifferent teachers, and that the quality of teaching needs to be vigilantly monitored. But that control should be exercised in the context of making the education system as a whole more democratic (for teachers as well) and more accountable — not just to HMIs and industrialists, but also to parents and students. One of the most objectionable features in some of Keith Joseph's proposals for teacher training is the way they sneak ideological criteria in through the back door of assessing professional competence. No teaching is ideologically innocent, but the aims, methods and outcomes of different pedagogies should be debated in public, not outlawed by ministerial fiat.

Similarly, the standards defined and imposed through the organization of the curriculum should be constantly scrutinized and challenged. What values are embedded in Scruton's 'recognized academic disciplines', for example? What is implied by their imposition on schools through the increasingly centralized control of the curriculum by the DES? What changes in the content of the curriculum — and also in the institutional forms, social relations and political control of schooling — would be necessary to develop *our* values? That is really the crucial question, for in defining those values — the dissemination of intellectual skills as part of a new common sense; the possibility and desirability of change; a popular democratic national culture — we would at the same time be constructing an achievable vision of the future.

Having taken Roger Scruton as our interlocutor, we should perhaps finish with him. He does at least follow through the logic of his arguments. 'It is not possible to provide universal education,' he concludes. 'Nor, indeed, is it desirable.' Education, as a privilege and a value, is useful and available only to a limited community of scholars. Others, not to be despised, require different civil institutions to prepare them for their humbler lot. In such arguments, Scruton represents a new but growing tendency in Conservative thinking. He does not just object to the expense of universal schooling, but to the very principle. Alongside the moves already instituted to privatize parts of educational provision and to restrict large sections of the population to merely manual training, its logic would be to make Britain the first country to renounce universal education. (For that reason alone, it would not become government policy. But, for the first time, the question is on the agenda — and the unthinkable has happened before.) The left's response should not be to hark back nostalgically to a fleeting, illusory moment when comprehensive schooling seemed to promise universal access to an already threadbare culture. Nor should it be to produce escapist curricular blueprints for an unrealizable socialist Nirvana. The strategic question that needs to be thought through is this: how do education and cultural struggle fit into a movement for socialist transformation? This movement, it now seems clear, may well be won or lost within the sphere of civil society. In 1961, Raymond Williams concluded his chapter on education in *The Long Revolution* like this:

> I do not doubt that the proposals suggested above will be called Utopian, but they are in fact the reverse. It is a question of whether we can grasp the real nature of our society, or whether we persist in social and educational patterns based on a limited ruling class, a middle professional class, a large operative class, cemented by forces that cannot be challenged and will not be changed. The privileges and barriers, of an inherited kind, will in any case go down. It is only a question of whether we replace them by the free play of the market, or by a public education designed to express and create the values of an educated democracy and a common culture.

More than 20 years later, that question remains frighteningly open.

11. Missing: a policy on the curriculum

Geoff Whitty

Critics of comprehensive school curricula sometimes claim the work is not sufficiently rigorous; sometimes they claim it is not sufficiently relevant. If pressed, they will often say that it is insufficiently rigorous for those going on to higher education and insufficiently relevant for the mass of the future workforce. Recent Conservative policies use this thinking to justify the development of a more rigid division between academic and pre-vocational streams in comprehensive schools. In the long term, this division may be institutionalized into separate forms of schooling again. Rarely does debate go beyond these alternatives: *either* an academic curriculum along the lines of that provided by traditional grammar schools *or* a narrowly instrumental and pre-vocational one. Other alternatives are hardly ever considered. Even the limited attempts to break out of this mould on the part of progressive teachers and curriculum development agencies in the 1960s and 1970s have been systematically misrepresented and marginalized — including, ironically, some designed to help in the regeneration of Britain's industrial performance.

The Labour Party leadership, too, has helped to sustain the conventional wisdom, traditionally adopting the view that a grammar school curriculum should be made available to all before switching its allegiance during the Great Debate to a pre-vocational model. Even those in the party who have doubts about such strategies have too often argued that questions about curricula, pedagogy and assessment can be sorted out only when we have finally achieved a completely comprehensive institutional structure. This has left us in recent years with a system of secondary education which most people believe to be comprehensive but whose curriculum in no sense deserves that label. What exists in many comprehensive schools is an uneasy compromise between academic and pre-vocational models of education which satisfies no one and breeds the sort of dissatisfaction that Conservatives can mobilize in support of their reactionary policies.

When we look at both the form and content of the prevailing curriculum models, it is clear that neither the academic nor the pre-vocational approach as currently conceived serves the interests that the labour movement ought to be promoting. Indeed, it is scarcely surprising that working-class groups, blacks and women have gained little of value from exposure to such curricula. The academic curriculum reflects what Raymond Williams calls a 'selective tradition' and represents the traditional culture of an elite as the only worthwhile knowledge. White upper- and middle-class male exploits dominate school history even today, while other groups are relegated to the sidelines and are seen to take a relatively passive part in events. Recent limited moves towards a greater emphasis on labour history, women's history and black history are now being condemned by conservative critics as diluting and distorting 'our' cultural heritage! So much of the academic curriculum still derives from the cultural experience of a ruling minority within which vast numbers of pupils find little meaningful to relate to. Its very emphasis on separate academic subjects apparently divorced from each other and from the world outside school makes it difficult for pupils to use this curriculum to gain a critical purchase on the world in which they live. Such a curriculum thus helps, at least by default, to maintain existing social arrangements and their attendant inequalities and injustices.

But the pre-vocational model that is gaining increasing legitimacy in the lower status parts of our comprehensive schools, and is now being promoted by the MSC, is not the answer either. Not only does it still remain a 'second-best' for those adjudged to be failures in terms of academic criteria, it too encourages acceptance of the status quo. Many courses have the effect of making existing forms of work and work-discipline appear natural rather than demonstrating the extent to which they are the product of a fundamentally unjust and in-egalitarian system. Though such courses sometimes seem more meaningful to pupils than the academic alternative, they are predominantly in the business of social control rather than social criticism. Many of the special courses now being introduced to cope with rising youth unemployment contain the implicit message that unemployment is the fault of the individuals rather than the system that creates it. Of course, the very term 'pre-vocational' has an ironic, even cynical, ring to it at a time of mass unemployment and the destruction and deskilling of occupations. For girls, the domesticating function of this part of the curriculum is particularly stark as they still find themselves guided towards options that prepare them for work in the home and only for traditionally 'female' jobs outside it. Though socialists and feminists sometimes take heart from evidence of growing pupil resistance to such courses, this cannot of itself be regarded as an adequate substitute for the development of a positive alternative strategy.

Tory policy on public examinations highlights the division between academic and pre-vocational schooling. For all the rhetoric about new forms of curriculum control and accountability, the examination system remains the single most important means of controlling the curriculum of English secondary schools. In current proposals for the future of 16-plus examinations, it is clear that the universities' traditional model of academic education will continue to dominate that part of the curriculum that leads to such examinations. This seems likely to be the case whether the existing GCE and CSE division remains or the proposed common examination actually gets off the ground. The CSE boards have already retreated from some of the more radical innovations that they sponsored in the 1960s and early 1970s so that they may now be judged as respectable, in conventional terms, as the GCE boards.

The academic bias in the proposed subject criteria for the new examination is now being used to justify the government's insistence that the exam should cater for only 60 per cent of the age-group — despite the fact that, in the past, the CSE boards have demonstrated the artificiality of such a division. This will allow the government, aided by the MSC, to sponsor a much narrower instrumental and pre-vocational approach for the remaining 40 per cent. Similarly, in 16—19 education, the extremely narrow but academically oriented 'A' level system favoured by the universities is to be retained, while the new lower-level 17-plus qualification is to be defined largely by bodies closely allied to industry and commerce.

Some trade unionists have tried to argue that the only way of resolving the continuing divisiveness represented in such developments, and of helping the recovery of British industry in the process, is to espouse the cause of pre-vocational education for all as an alternative to academic education for all. This is also a view held by some industrialists who argue that much of the failure of British industry is to be put at the door of the elitist and irrelevant education to which its future managers are subjected, a form of education which they argue also turns away from industry many of those people who in other countries might be attracted to it. Even Thatcherism, arguably less attached to traditional ruling-class culture than earlier forms of Conservatism, has yet to grasp this nettle. But, for the left, the concern should not be to revive and celebrate industry in its present form but to transform it so that it serves the interests of those it currently exploits. If the attraction of pre-vocational education lies in its grasp of relevance and meaningfulness in education, its disadvantage lies in its uncritical approach to the status quo. On the other hand, the elements of critique and rigour which some people argue are central to the academic curriculum are rarely actually used to probe the assumed merits of current social arrangements.

What has to be faced is that neither of the prevailing curriculum models will adequately serve the needs of the disadvantaged groups within our present society. A genuinely comprehensive curriculum needs to be both meaningful *and* critical and to ensure that its definitions of relevance and rigour are not ones that relate only to the culture and interests of those who at root support an inegalitarian society. The academic tradition stems essentially from the curriculum of nineteenth-century public schools designed to perpetuate an elite; the pre-vocational model is essentially a variant of the nineteenth-century elementary tradition designed to control rather than emancipate the masses. Yet even socialist support for mass access to elementary education in the nineteenth-century and to secondary education in the twentieth has often been accompanied by an uncritical attitude towards the sort of education pupils are to gain access to. Alternative traditions, including some interesting socialist alternatives outside the state system, have rarely informed the labour movement's policy on the content and control of state provision. Important as it is to defend state education as something from which disadvantaged groups can potentially gain, it is equally important not to defend the indefensible. Present approaches to curricula, pedagogy and assessment too often fall into this category. They must now be subjected to critical scrutiny and, where found inappropriate, contested. This is not to suggest that all aspects of existing curricular arrangements should be written off because of their social origins. It is to suggest that the value of many of them to working-class students has too often been taken for granted by the left.

One of the reasons why the left has given so little thought to the nature of the curriculum is that it has often held the view, at least in the post-war period, that such matters are best left to teachers. The Great Debate and subsequent attacks on teacher control over curricula and examinations have helped to put under strain the tacit understandings that existed about this between the teaching profession and the labour movement. Yet this need not necessarily have been an entirely reactionary development. It has effectively become that because the left has made no distinctive contribution to the debates about alternatives to conventional notions of teacher professionalism. While other groups in the community have been quick to make their own claims upon the school curriculum, the left has failed to develop, in conjunction with the political constituencies whose interests it claims to represent, a sense of a present-day equivalent of what nineteenth-century radicals dubbed '*really* useful knowledge'. This would presumably include an exploration of ways in which social injustices and inequalities could be investigated, questioned and eventually transformed. Some − though by no means all − of the progressive and radical innovations of the 1960s and early 1970s themselves took this as their project. Yet, partly because the teachers involved often had no real political base outside the profession and took little trouble to develop one, their work was easily marginalized. In any future alliance between teachers and other social groups curriculum issues need to be matters of open discussion and collaboration from the start.

Clearly the development of a distinctive but popular socialist position on the curriculum would not ensure its establishment as the mainstream curriculum of the state educational system. Nevertheless, if the left were to develop and mobilize around a clearer view of what such a curriculum might involve, it would at least have a chance of substantially influencing the outcome of current debates on the issue. Ignoring them or giving uncritical support to any of the existing views of the curriculum can only ensure that the system will never even begin to serve the interests of those ill-served by existing arrangements. There are, however, some aspects even of today's generally bleak educational scene that give grounds for cautious optimism about the effects that a coherent intervention from the left might have. The idea that it is possible to create a form of curriculum that combines rigour and relevance is at least as appealing as the idea that the solution to disillusion with the current situation is greater division between them. The concern from both sides of industry about the nature and effects of existing academic curricula could lead to more support for such a development than might initially be expected. In addition, the effect of falling school rolls on school curricula is likely to be devastating in the next few years. In some schools, the very idea of a curriculum based upon discrete subjects may not remain viable for much longer. Multi-disciplinary and integrated programmes may thus become a necessity. Whatever the failings of some of these programmes in the past, at their best they can offer considerably more space than conventional curricular arrangements for examining the nature of the disciplines and using them to explore meaningful issues in a systematic and critical way. In this situation, the choice between rigour and relevance can be exposed as an unnecessary one and one that no longer needs to bedevil discussion of the content and organization of the curriculum.

Indeed, if discussions about a core curriculum involved major rethinking along these lines, rather than just seeking to identify which existing subjects should be in or out, then they could be a potentially progressive development. Yet the potential in all such situations has to be activated and this is why the left needs to develop and mobilize around policies on these issues. The same is true of other recent initiatives such as political education, multi-racial education and equal opportunities policies. Though increasingly treated with suspicion by conservatives as they gain confidence to pursue even more reactionary policies, these initiatives have ironically themselves often been conservative in their effects. Yet they need not necessarily be so. Here again, the experience of individual teachers and groups of teachers in developing critical consciousness and in fostering anti-sexist and anti-racist policies within their schools demonstrates the radical possibilities inherent within such attempts to change the curriculum. The recent initiatives by the Inner London Education Authority on class, gender and race and on political education take this process one stage further. Nevertheless, their achievements to date and some of the responses to them show just how entrenched conventional views of the curriculum are and how much change is going to be necessary if constructive new working relationships are to be developed between educational professionals and those sections of the wider community that have traditionally been excluded from curricular decision-making.

What is needed now if further progress is to be made is a recognition that such work must be more clearly integrated into a broader programme of political reconstruction on the left. Some of the policies the left has supported in the past *are* difficult to justify and may even, in a few cases, deserve to succumb to reactionary attacks on them. The responsibility of the left in the years ahead is to develop and fight for policies that are defensible and relate to the concerns of those groups that the selective tradition in English education has never really served. It is a challenge we have neglected for far too long.

12. Moral order and discipline

AnnMarie Wolpe

Central to Thatcherism is the assertion that our economic and social problems are due largely to a decline in the moral order of society. This decline, it is said, is manifested in the disintegration of family life, and in truancy, vandalism, violence and selfishness amongst youth. Indeed Dr Rhodes Boyson* has 'no doubt that there is 1,000 per cent increase in adolescent violence in the last eighteen years' and this he blames on the failure of schools.

These are complex questions and quite clearly the social problems to which Dr Boyson refers, such as violence and vandalism, do give cause for worry and the need for something to be done. However, Dr Boyson's linking these problems directly with a value system is incorrect. Neither is the way in which he introduces disciplinary issues at all helpful. On the other hand, oppositional forces have failed either to recognize or deal effectively with these questions and their specific relationship to discipline in regard to the educational system. This particular omission needs to be rectified both in terms of acknowledgement of the situation and in the formulation of concrete measures to deal with it. These then are the central concerns of this article.

In an effort to reverse the asserted decay of the moral order the Conservatives have over the past 4 years adopted a number of strategies, particularly relating to the legal system, the family and education. For example, prior to his removal from office, William Whitelaw, former Home Secretary, in order to combat what he saw as the erosion of law and order, introduced significant changes in the criminal code and the nature of punishment meted out to juveniles, and had been engaged in a struggle to extend, quite alarmingly, the

---

* Unless otherwise stated the quotations from Dr Boyson are taken from his book, *The Crisis in Education*, The Woburn Press, 1975.

powers of the police. But this is not the only area which is considered essential by the Conservatives for intervention. Defects in the moral code may be fought in the fields of education and through the family. Plans are afoot to re-establish what is seen as the lost, but still appropriate values of our society through restoring the proper role of family life. This will influence children through strict up-bringing and the inculcation of correct moral values. The family has declined because of the failure of parents to be 'real' parents, which in Dr Boyson's terms refers to the 'real' world where father goes out to work and mother is a 'real mother' (p.51).

In conformity with the right's thinking and their indifference to the fate of approximately one in six families entirely dependent on the earnings of a single parent — inevitably a woman's — Dr Boyson advocates the exclusion of women from the workforce. This would help to overcome the defects among young people who are 'brought up to be selfish, pleasure seeking, irresponsible, etc. Everywhere there was a cry for rights and the breakdown of structures.' But parents are also more generally at fault, reflecting the 'self-centred hedonistic philosophy of the late 1960s' (the *Guardian*, 20 March 1983). And this brings education to the centre of Conservative strategy.

Dr Boyson identifies two main elements in the educational system which he says are responsible for the deterioration of moral order: the role of 'egalitarians' and the absence of discipline in the schools. These appear as inextricably linked as his arguments unfold.

'Excessive freedom and absence of firm discipline in our schools' are responsible for 'truancy, vandalism, and drug taking amongst our youth'. 'Egalitarians', we are told, 'are opposed to structure and curriculum' and encourage total anarchy. The ideas of the 'egalitarians' are responsible for the 'teachers, encouraged by their education authorities, going there as missionaries to preach a culture of liberation which has no meaning to the boys and which they spurn by violence and truancy.' (Of course to Dr Boyson the most important sector in education comprises boys: he does not seem to recognize the existence of girls within our schools!) But teachers are also victims, according to Dr Boyson, in that child-centred education has 'led to deprived children, lower standards, disorderly classrooms, and defenceless and disillusioned teachers'.

To combat the insidious influence of 'egalitarians' Dr Boyson says there must be a return to a discipline and to the 'clear and confident virtues of the Victorian State'. The virtues would include Samuel Smiles's notion of self-help, the Protestant work ethic, and the 'Arnoldian concept of a tradition of literature, art and ideas', which represent a 'high culture', as contrasted with what he sees as the 'inferior culture' of the working classes.

As becomes apparent from the above, the two elements — the ideology of equality, and the absence of discipline — are firmly interlocked according to Dr Boyson's way of thinking. Yet if one takes his arguments at all seriously, then a number of difficulties become immediately apparent.

In the first place Dr Boyson adopts an ahistorical position which is surprising given that he himself is an historian. Dr Boyson fails to recognize the appalling social problems which existed in the Victorian era. He only draws attention nostalgically to a Golden Age. He makes no mention of the extremes of poverty, the high levels of crime, prostitution, adolescent deviancy, and appalling levels of health. Pornography became a lucrative though covert industry catering for the sexual fantasies of the heads of respectable households. The religious dogma of the state of grace effectively legitimated the hardships endured by the masses, and the notion of original sin justified the punitive treatment, including brutal corporal punishment, meted out to school children, boys and girls alike. The Victorian era certainly did hold virtues of industriousness and self-help and thrift; it also generated and was responsible for extensive cruelties and inequalities in the society.

In the second instance he never clarifies what comprises 'egalitarianism'. The term is used pejoratively: labelling someone as an egalitarian appears sufficient cause, in Dr Boyson's eyes, to justify steps which would effectively remove them from the educational scene. Because somebody adopts an ideological position which argues for equal opportunities it simply does not follow that that person opposes 'structure' within a school or, even more ludicrously, the operation of a curriculum, as Dr Boyson would have us believe. This is pure nonsense, and amounts to little more than a smear campaign. Educationalists on the left *are* very much concerned with structures, the form they take and what comprises the curriculum.

Dr Boyson's ideas about what constitutes values, how they come into being and the extent of their effectiveness, also turn out to be both simplistic and empiricist. According to him a single factor, discipline, can itself create a complex set of values. He ignores the multi-faceted nature of values and how they are generated. He also ignores the possibility that simply because certain values are preached, they will also be universally practised. Take his Victorian era again. Its idealized images of the family or individual behaviour bore little relation to the way most people lived their lives.

The nature and structure of discipline in Dr Boyson's account are far from straightforward. Discipline he sees as a hierarchically ordered, highly differentiated, authoritarian system which maintains rigid divisions.

In his ideal society mothers are at home all day, and schools are highly disciplined. Individualism, as contrasted with collective action, is prized, and would guarantee the inculcation of appropriate values into a compliant and docile youth who would unquestioningly fit into the demands of the labour market. Teachers would be trained to espouse the ideals he cherishes, they would certainly not be concerned with inequalities. The system would cater for the elite and there would be control over what constitutes knowledge. In the name of establishing a moral order he is, consequently, able to justify drastic education cuts and amongst other things control over teacher training.

His attack, like the right's, on the absence of discipline and poor moral order have had unintended consequences on the left's way of reacting to such issues. We have tended to ignore such issues even though we are fully aware that discipline is a matter that needs to be confronted. This is due largely to a tendency by both progressive people and the left to equate discipline with authoritarianism. In order not to be tainted by the label of 'authoritarianism' the left has turned a blind eye to some of the questionable aspects of libertarian policies and has avoided recognition of the relation of discipline to social problems within schools. We know perfectly well that schools reflect the social conditions of the wider society, and what factors contribute to these. We know how pupils react and the form their alienation takes. But we also need to consider and assess the role of discipline as both a short-term and a long-term measure in order to produce an effective educational system. Forms of discipline do play a crucial role in the learning process, it is an essential feature in classroom practice and its potential in regard to democratization should not be underestimated.

It is clear from all that has been said that the term discipline has been used by Dr Boyson in two distinct contexts: one relates to processes involved in forms of social control, and the other as effecting conduct considered appropriate in terms of moral issues. Dr Boyson tends to collapse both meanings and use the terms interchangeably, a practice which leads to confusion and a clouding of issues. There are, of course, other meanings attached to the term discipline and these include formal instruction, a specialism or department of knowledge, as well as several religious connotations. In the following discussion, the term discipline is used primarily in regard to rules and regulations which prescribe the parameters of socially accepted forms of behaviour. These rules may be overtly stated as, for example, the wearing of school uniform, or may be less consciously stated but encapsulated in the form learning takes within the institutional setting. It is important to realize that these rules and regulations are not fixed but are closely linked to social conditions and so subject to change.

Beginning with the interrelation between learning and discipline, we know that part of children's development involves self-discipline. But this does not automatically ensure that children will willingly learn those parts of the curriculum regarded as important and essential. Certain strategies have been devised to ensure this form of social control, and the most successful is the examination system. Obviously examinations operate in an effective way in those schools where they are the order of the day, with high academic reputations and with pupils matched to this type of expectation. But for a significant proportion of pupils this form of discipline does not operate for the simple reason that they do not anticipate, and indeed will never attempt, any public examinations. This applies not only to those overtly disaffected pupils whose opposition to school is manifest in so many ways, but also to those quieter, non-overtly oppositional pupils — and this includes so many female pupils — who leave school without gaining any qualifications. The cause of this is multi-faceted, but in considering the so-called failure of so many pupils, the role of discipline — particularly in regard to pupils' commitment to learning and self-development — should be recognized. Alternatives to the examination system should be investigated and these must go beyond the usual plea of making education more 'relevant'.

There are aspects of discipline which relate to the daily rules and regulations which assume a ritualistic form in schools. These, while arguably necessary, are nevertheless unable to eradicate the cause for malcontent in the schools. Furthermore, these rituals are often imposed in an authoritarian form which negates any possibility of obtaining the full co-operation of all concerned. This clearly is an area in which some form of democratization could occur without losing sight of the purposes of such rituals.

Then there is classroom control: here individual technique and experience of the teachers are important. But because teachers, including head teachers, are judged on the basis of their ability to keep order, they are under pressure never to admit to any difficulties within their own classrooms. Such admission is equated with overall failure. This is not to suggest that most teachers are unable to maintain control in the classroom, nor that they are themselves unaware of the problems; indeed, many experiment with different forms of classroom control. Nevertheless, much could be learned from broadly based discussions which would locate classroom practice within wider parameters that recognized the numerous factors that contribute to the maintenance of a successful classroom.

Another element, and probably one of the most contentious, relates disciplinary issues to the democratization process. Here I take democratic practices to refer to the assumption of responsibility. When discussing this in relation to pupils it refers to responsibility which goes beyond their individual concern, and embraces the wider group. Nor does this mean 'crying for rights', as Dr Boyson suggested, or the call for participation in determining, say, what should or should not be taught, which after all is the province of educationalists. Democratization is not tied in with authoritarian regimes: it could generate a productive atmosphere in which learning, in the fullest meaning of the word, could take place. Learning democratic procedures at school can certainly contribute to a greater participation in these activities as adults, but this can only occur within a situation in which socially prescribed rules and regulations are observed.

To speak of discipline in isolation from the different elements in the learning process and its role in development of democratic procedures is to devalue the meaning and role of education. We are not concerned with discipline as a form of authoritarian control. We cannot accept Dr Boyson's notion of discipline as an excuse to validate the cutbacks, an attack on progressive ideas, and an attempt to relegate women to the kitchen sink. We need to consider very seriously the problems surrounding the functioning of discipline within our schools in order to begin to meet some of the many problems of contemporary society. Education plays a major part in the development of the individual for full citizenship, and discipline is but one part of the whole process. Dr Boyson is right to stress the relevance of discipline, but for completely the wrong reasons. Finally, whilst appropriate disciplinary procedures can contribute to a well-ordered, creative and productive learning environment, it is totally false to assume that they will in themselves create a 'good' moral order. Values are not derived from disciplinary procedures but from the broadly based cultural formations in the wider society.

13. Independence and accountability for all

Caroline Benn

One of the staples of British education is the left's claim that 'doing something' about private schools is a top priority, while in fact nothing is ever done.

In no field is rhetoric easier to come by. From the 1920s, when Tawney demolished private education in debate, none has attracted more plans or promises. In the mid-1960s, when the Labour Party's policy was integration, Labour even set up a royal commission. It sat for years and produced predictably unacceptable recommendations: too weak for the socialist left, too strong for the conservative right. Only one was ever enacted — the withdrawal of a yearly grant to a few fee-paying schools in 1974, ironically increasing private school numbers by about 150.

As one Labour manifesto succeeded another, the sections on 'doing something' degenerated steadily until only a token stand against charity status remained. Yet nothing was ever done about charity status, and after Labour's 1979 defeat the old round started up again with a new working party, a new report setting out exactly why any government of the left must deal with the issue of private education, and a promise of a fresh attempt.

This is thus a good time for the left to look at this issue with new eyes.

First, to see that public schools are only one part of the independence issue, albeit still crucial. For from only a small handful come most of those who really own and run society: the majority of the big private landowners, senior civil servants, military officers, lawyers and judges and other key professionals, bankers and directors of big industry, the senior ranks of the media and the state church. What's more, the monopoly of these few schools on life's top chances — often through the filter of Oxbridge — is the same in the 1980s as it was in the 1930s. So much for the enormous changes that are supposed to have taken place.

Other advanced industrial countries also have elite educational institutions, but these have a wider social base and nowadays are almost all at graduate or post-graduate level. Britain's are unique not just for their narrow middle-class base but because they start at secondary level — some say as early as 8, when prep schools recruit.

Guarding this core of social power is always top priority in any conservative education strategy, and explains why Britian has been unable to accept the change to comprehensive education which other countries — both capitalist and communist — accepted much more easily. To others it was an inevitable development, the desired accompaniment of rising living standards which required postponement of differentiation to the mid-teens in order to give the general population a wider knowledge base.

In Britain, however, it became a social rather than an educational issue. In the resulting struggle public schools were too weak to stand on their own and allied with state grammar schools to defend 'standards', 'freedom' and 'choice' — all three words carefully defined by those controlling public debate to mean the privileged positions of both. Black Paper campaigners, recruited equally from private and selective education, provided up-front agitation, and relied on the media for supportive propaganda.

The *Times* set the ball rolling in 1965 by inciting opposition to comprehensive change on the grounds that the 'middle-classes' must 'insist' on keeping their 'own schools' for the transmission of their 'own manners, codes, attitudes, ideas and learning'. Yet it was the left which was branded as playing politics with education, even though at no time did socialists urge the working-class to regard comprehensive schools as 'theirs', or incite the majority to fight the elite for their own educational rights. Perhaps this is exactly what has always been missing from the left's policy.

The system froze

The result of education's politicization on the right's terms was that educational development was not addressed and even the most basic reforms languished: curriculum change, teacher education, and vocational preparation — to name but three. The educational establishment couldn't even agree to let go of the narrow and outworn 'A' level, despite three separate attempts, so paralysed was it by its own contradictory campaign to restrict entry to life's chances against what it had been made to believe was an educational rabble pressing at the gates.

Throughout this time when so little was really changing, people were being told that tradition was being jettisoned, that extremists were in control and that everything was about to collapse from untried experiments. The truth was that Labour was attempting a long overdue reform and had been blown off political course by the late 1960s. By 1976 Labour was clinging to a new conservative consensus, the left never having had its chance to come out fighting for its own constituents: that majority whom education had neglected for so long.

That majority, however, felt the neglect. Unfortunately, their justified dissatisfaction, fuelled by false propaganda as to its cause, sometimes went to resisting the very changes which would have provided them with the rights they were seeking. It even drove a few to try to 'buy' opportunities — which should have been theirs already — in unpowerful or wholly inadequate private schools.

All during this period, the powerful private schools were insisting quite hysterically that they were about to be destroyed by education ministers, when, of course, none ever tried to take anything other than token action against any of them. However, their well-oiled public relations machinery mobilized their adherents. Private capital — at last count about £40million a year from industry alone — helped public schools beat inflation, which was their only real threat.

It was a wonderful confidence trick on both sides, however unintentional, and guaranteed that development in the fee paying sector (where there has been no genuine innovation since A.S.Neill) froze even more solidly than in the state, where at least several progressive currents have made substantial headway. Nowadays, when private schools brag about modernizing they are apt to mention practices which were standard in elementary schools a hundred years ago: girls educated alongside boys, technical training, or accepting pupils in their own clothes.

Independent schools become 'dependent schools'

Meanwhile, in the 1970s a much bigger confidence trick was just coming to light with the discovery of how heavy a financial burden ratepayers and taxpayers bear to keep private education going for the benefit of a tiny minority, mostly highly advantaged already, and how slyly these schools are being used to undermine the majority's struggling new comprehensive system.

A key practice has always been 'place-buying', whereby, incredibly, the general public pay the private school fees for certain privileged parents — like diplomats and military officers. Lesser members of these callings, like ordinary enlisted personnel, have far fewer perks. These payments to private education quietly grew in the 1960s and 1970s, as other groups tried to claim they too 'travelled', or had specially gifted children or 'desired' boarding as a way of life. Some found comprehensives unsuitable, sometimes it was just class snobbery pure and simple. The Victorian warning that the 'gently brought up' child would be 'infected' by education alongside working-class pupils in comprehensives was not written in 1870 but in a Black Paper in 1970.

In effect, private school place-buying was being used to replace the grammar option that had always been available to the minority. Those taking it up, however, were even more narrowly middle-class than the general grammar population by this time, and much narrower than the old grammar population of the 1950s.

In many local authorities — usually Conservative controlled — the expenditure ran into millions, all at a time when falling pupil numbers left empty places already paid for in state schools. The loss of resources, both financial and human — those paid for twice over were almost all potential sixth-formers — unbalanced and demoralized the new comprehensives and stunted their growth. In some areas where these arrangements were being made, there was no discussion at the elected education committee. Agreement was reached behind closed doors by education officials and the private schools themselves.

Eventually, people began to add up the sums. Direct taxpayer subsidy was nearly £200million a year by the end of the 1970s. Indirect subsidies were far higher: tax concessions for fee-paying parents; tax reliefs for private schools classed as charities, who often pay no rates on extensive properties; money for new types of state private schools, like European Schools; money for services to the private system from the state, like educational exchange arrangements; money for holiday travel fares for private school pupils, including air fares. Including money for special education and money to educate and train the teachers who teach in private schools, the total bill is now approaching £500million a year.

Although no public debate was permitted in the mass media on this issue, the odd item slipped out. Many began to ask questions — not only about the huge public cost, but also why private schools were so unaccountable to their local areas. They also wanted to know why so often choices went to those from families who were already so manifestly advantaged. Working-class children's needs to board were never looked at seriously; gypsy children were never offered thousands each year because their parents travelled. When working-class families were uprooted from the inner cities and sent to outlying council estates, no one funded their children to continue at their existing schools until the leaving age. On the other hand, when middle-class parents went broke, local authorities — including Labour's ILEA up to the middle of the 1970s — regularly picked up their private school bills to keep continuity for their children.

As the mechanism and deleterious results of middle-class manipulation became clear, Labour authorities began to stop buying places. They asked for national subsidies to be replaced by equitable arrangements that did not threaten comprehensive schools. This merely drew yet another ineffective circular from a dithering government, soon to be defeated.

In 1979 the Conservatives swept in and within a year had passed two major education acts in contrast to Labour who had not passed one in 11 years of government. Conservatives, who had attacked Labour endlessly for trying to 'force' comprehensives on a handful of unwilling local authorities (when Labour had never even legislated to end selection), immediately forced more place-buying on every local authority in the land. It took the form of an 'assisted places' scheme, which will give the private schools at least £50million more a year, and cream the average comprehensive sixth form of half its university-bound pupils.

It was bitterly opposed by all shades of opinion. But it was too late. The same legislation protected the privileged's right to continue manipulating parental choice everywhere else in the system as well. The old 11-plus, which at least had been a universal and open practice, re-emerged as a covert and optional one, cleverly hidden in what appeared to be legal rights all could enjoy. In fact, as was soon discovered, 'choice' of both grammar school and private schools was available only to those parents who had wealth or whose children had passed attainment tests at an earlier age than others. Exactly as it had always been.

Except that selection was now law, and that this time one of its major objectives was the preservation of the old private education. Both legally and financially the state has extended its powers to keep private privilege alive, and few are yet really aware of just how extensive the cover is. Nearly 500 schools, including every major public school, are listed in *Hansard* as receiving public payment for diplomats' children, and over 1,100 are on the military payroll. Those few private schools not on either receive local funding or have parents with tax concessions.

In other words, almost every private secondary school now has a public subsidy of some sort – some a very large one. And every year ratepayers and taxpayers are going to be asked to shift more public money from the majority's own public education service into the minority's private one. Objectionable enough in the best of times, it is intolerable when the public's own education service is being cut, run down, and sold off to private bidders in search of private profits.

Under the Conservatives, 'independent' schools are getting more dependent each year. It is highly doubtful if any genuinely independent secondary schools exist any more at all. Far-seeing Conservatives deplore this, fearing that further extension of such support give the majority a clear right to decide how private education shall develop in future. Perhaps this is a right we should have been claiming all along?

The dilemmas of right and left

Conservatives are certainly well aware of the dangers in their policy and for this reason will now seek to widen the class base of private education. This has always been the traditional way to protect elite schooling. Adding a few working-class pupils disarms criticism and at the same time draws off potential working-class leaders to identify with middle-class interests. When this is done — preferably with fanfare — Conservatives can revert to their favourite myth that all direct grant grammar schools were always full of road-sweepers' sons and daughters.

The problem for the right is that the only means acceptable to private education for accomplishing this is some form of selection, preferably academic. Yet if there is one thing proven after 40 years of selection — and shown repeatedly in census, DES statistics or the Public Schools Commission's own research — it is that selection reinforces middle-class advantage. It is also known that selection destroys the schools from which selected pupils come, which is why any proposals for private education's collaboration with the state sector are also doomed. In the long run they always entail some form of creaming of the state's resources: 'Heads private education always wins, tails comprehensives always lose.' Only a relationship which abides by the comprehensive principle will be acceptable in the long term, and everyone knows this. In many ways, therefore, private education is now the right's problem.

Meanwhile, the left has problems enough of its own, one of which is Labour's private schools' policy, embarrassing in its richness: end all subsidies; continue subsidies on certain conditions; stop charity status; allow charity status on certain conditions; integrate locally through LEA planning; incorporate nationally through a central plan.

Any one proposal might have its good points but all would depend on first developing a genuinely comprehensive education policy that had merit — and which the left, at all levels, was prepared to argue with confidence and enthusiasm. Until we have a clear idea of the way we want education overall to develop, any separate policy for private education would be dictated by private school interests — not the needs of the community as a whole.

This comprehensive interest must come first. Only when we insist on having this debate — and have been allowed by the media to air the issues involved in continual public discussion — can people come to any meaningful conclusion about how to use the community's resources, including schools, whether fee-paying or not. Ending fee-paying is not a policy, it is what would follow when we had a policy that was clearly popular because people could see, directly, how they would benefit.

Until then, people will just have to live with yet more 'big lie' propaganda that preserving privilege for the few is somehow a 'freedom' for them, and will make up for the educational injustice, inferior provision, and lack of choice that in the present system they are condemned to go on experiencing for themselves and their children.

The left's myths

Meanwhile, the left could help by shifting its own myths, one of which is that all private schools are clones of Eton. The private sector is varied, with individuality in style and size and the extent to which schools are open to the world outside. A few − the free ones − are already non-feepaying neighbourhood comprehensive schools, with much experience to contribute.

Another is that private education is all about children, when many − perhaps most − private educational concerns are busy dispensing a rather narrow range of courses to adults, particularly those in the business and industrial world. Some of these institutions are responsible and innovative; many are offering shoddy goods at inflated prices.

Recently, the problem has escalated with the proliferation of colleges crowding around the Manpower Services Commission for funds to train young people in the very limited range of skills associated with the Youth Training Scheme. While they are given these lucrative contracts, public sector further education courses − often of real quality − are being destroyed for ever. The result, quite intentionally, is to shift yet more millions away from the state sector into the private. But here the response could well be different: the spectacle of clever cowboy-college operators making vast personal profits, now an open secret, could well be just what will fuel public opinion to demand we 'do something' about private education, and insist that the high standards and accountability of state education be enforced in the private sector too.

Such a development would be necessary in any case if we are serious about life-long education after 18. This requires many new venues as well as widening the services and programmes in many public institutions — some of which, like universities, still insist on being treated as if they were independent and shared nothing in common with local colleges or polytechnics. All post-18 education will eventually have to be brought under the same kind of democratic control which we are presently insisting that schools accept.

But note carefully that we only insist on this for certain schools. We do not insist on it for fee-paying schools, even when taxpayers and ratepayers are picking up ever more of their bill. Nor do we expect special schools for special needs to be included. Such schools are often classed as private — even when the public buys 100 per cent of the places. Even the Labour Party's private school policy excludes them from its plans — a very odd and potentially unpopular proposal at a time when integrating pupils with special needs into mainstream education is so widely advocated.

Perhaps the largest group of schools in a grey and complex area of accountability are the voluntary schools, mostly religious in foundation. Most co-operate very well with the local authority which maintains them, their erstwhile financial independence is all but gone today. A few, however, insist on behaving as laws unto themselves, educationally and organizationally, and have lately come to public attention because of opposition within a developing comprehensive system to the way they are misusing their status to keep on selecting — socially, academically, and racially.

Because such lack of accountability began to incur what the churches cannot afford — hostility from the larger school community — progressive members of the religions involved have started internal reforms. Their conservative counterparts, however, have insisted on protecting educational privilege; in the 1980 Education Act this was provided by the Conservative government. It simply prolongs the problem.

The left has often dodged the religious issue by hiding behind the undeniably preferable ideological position of opposition to schools segregated on any basis. But one-third of our schools are already segregated by religion. What is more unavoidable, members of religions other than Roman Catholic and Church of England, including ethnic minority religions, are asking why they cannot have their own schools, too. The left has to offer something more than a refusal to have more voluntary schools, or a promise to harmonize the practices of those which already exist with their neighbouring county schools — necessary though both such policies are.

There must be some positive recognition that different groups have a right to regard schools as 'their own' and to find in them — or other public services — time and space and means to study their religion or further their own cultures. The system also has to find a way to allow groups which think they have been systematically denied in education, like certain black communities, or groups of girls, to undertake their own extra activity — provided the general community of schools agree. Having to spend privately is not a solution, but a symptom.

Seeing it differently

The problem is not private versus state. Rather, it is how a publicly funded education service can offer choice to all alike instead of one set of choices to a privileged few — while the majority are offered only a second-class opportunity at all stages. The problem is how to balance autonomy and accountability, individual initiative and collective advance.

All schools and colleges have to become accountable in the same way if we are ever to offer more equitable choices to everyone. But accountability that sacrifices autonomy too far should be unacceptable to the left. The missing part of so many previous attempts to 'do something' is any consideration of how to extend some of the benefits of independence to the many schools, particularly county schools, which don't have enough of it to develop fully. Provided all schools and colleges have the same degree of it, and that the democratically elected hold the ring, this could be a positive outcome with majority support.

There is no possibility of change, however, until the majority understand that education and life's chances ought not to be a middle-class monopoly. Change can only occur when the majority insist that education forward their own interests, including the diversity of their own 'codes, manners, attitudes, ideas and learning'. Spreading that understanding is our political task.

Part four

Teachers, parents and students

Introduction

The main headline in the *Daily Mirror* on 23 March 1983 was 'Shock issue: Save Our Schools'. The paper ran a number of special articles highlighting the crisis — a school built for a hundred pupils having to cope with 270 'boisterous boys and girls', schools with leaking roofs and damp classrooms, school buildings still in use half a century after being condemned, pupils unable to develop exceptional talents for lack of funding or specialist teachers, books out of date or simply falling to pieces. 'In the last Labour government's final year,' stated the *Mirror* editorial, '£500million *more* was spent on education than on defence. By 1985 the present government plans to spend £4,000million *less* on education than on defence.'

The National Association of Head Teachers, which represents more than two-thirds of the country's state school heads, is, according to a report in the *Guardian*, a 'traditionally conservative' organization. At its conference in June 1983, however, it bitterly attacked both the government's policies on education and also the leadership of Sir Keith Joseph.

Such examples indicate the range of potential support that exists for at least current levels of expenditure on education. But they also hint at some of the major obstacles to the effective mobilization of that support. In the first place, it is primarily a *defensive* response. That is a necessary first stage, of course. National and local campaigns against the running down or closure of schools are urgently needed, and can be built upon politically. But the danger is always that attacking the present disaster can imply a return to the ways things were before. It is clear that for the left this can no longer be an option. Massive, bureaucratic institutions, comprehensive in name only, have proved alienating for students, parents and teachers alike. They have failed to bring about the promised social changes. Too often they have been insensitive to the desires and aspirations of diverse communities and social groups.

This leads to the second difficulty — the conflicting interests of those who share a genuine concern for the quality of education. In its exposé, the *Mirror* was using the decay of schools as an indictment of Thatcherism and as part of a longer-term campaign for the return of Labour to power. The head teachers were making a professional case, that adequate resources were needed if they were to do their job properly. They were not questioning their own often autocratic powers.

The articles in this section have all been written by people who are directly involved in the educational process in one way or another. In that sense, they represent the perceptions and tactics of 'interested parties'. In any attempt to construct popular democratic alliances around education, the question of how — or indeed whether — these different interests can be forged together needs to be addressed directly. Traditionally, for example, teachers and parents have always been wary of each other. The institutional relationship between them makes that inevitable. Teachers want to exercise control over their own work; parents want a say in how their children are educated. Students, too, make their own demands on schooling, and different groups of students have different expectations. No identity of interests between teachers, parents and students can be assumed, therefore, but their different interests would have to be taken account of in defining new objectives and programmes. That means questioning traditional forms of activity and struggle, as well as the political and educational assumptions on which they are based. Trade union militancy among teachers or tinkering with the membership of governing bodies are not on their own sufficient. It will also be necessary to rethink and win the *educational* argument among teachers, among parents and also in the Labour Party.

The relationship between educational strategies and the politics of the Labour Party is of considerable importance in attempts to develop new strategies. Several of the articles here report how local initiatives, whether in anti-sexist and anti-racist teaching or in defending a school threatened with closure, can not only achieve a degree of success but also open up new political questions and possibilities. The problem then is how to translate such work into a *national* policy. The Labour Party at local, national and parliamentary level must be willing to do this.

Finally, in what is objectively a grim situation, it is worth underlining the remarkable successes that are achieved as a matter of routine within our schools. Education is not a panacea for deep-seated social and cultural inequalities and problems, and the failings and difficulties that exist must be faced. But a great deal can be achieved within it. Nothing would be more foolish or more damaging than to swallow the narrow-minded propaganda which seeks to destroy it.

14. Dear parent...

Anne Showstack Sassoon

'If at first you don't succeed, try, try again.'

Popular saying

'We are not considered competent enough for the courtesy of Annual School Reports any more.'

Parent quoted in Black Paper 1

'Most parents are frightened that if they make too much fuss, their children will suffer.'

Daily Mail, 18 January 1955

No right-wing campaign about education would have a chance of success if it did not relate in important ways to elements of popular experience. Although children and young people are the subjects and objects of education, the experience which is invoked by the right is that of the parent. The appeal is particularly effective because schools are outposts of the welfare state, involving a very large part of the population in daily contact. Not only does concern for their children's education strike an emotional chord in the parents, but schools are supposed both to account for themselves and to create a working relationship with parents. Schools are more open than other state institutions, and are markedly different from the world of work. This has not always been so, and it is the product of many battles not yet concluded which have produced new demands and new expectations amongst parents which the right has responded to in its fashion.

'Parent' is a blanket term leaving class, sex, and race unspecified. Millions of us think of ourselves as parents alongside our other identities, and certainly we are addressed as such by schools. When the right claims to represent the interest of parents it may obscure differences between them while emphasizing individualism — but that does not mean that the subject 'parents' does not exist. A parent has a particular kind of responsibility for and relationship to a child. To be a parent is to relate to the needs of a particular child or children and to do what is 'best' for them. 'Best' is determined purely by the fact of parenthood. At the same time a person is addressed as one amongst many parents by an institution and by people in that institution. The school relates to 'parents', rather than manual or white-collar workers, black or white people. With regard to sex, on the other hand, because it is overwhelmingly women who normally are in contact with the school, the image invoked is often the mother, at times the mother and father, but rarely the father as such.

A person's identity as a 'parent' is reinforced in several ways. In the first place parents relate in the main to teachers, and others such as educational psychologists all of whom are defined as specialized experts by training and work. That they, too, might be parents and/or black, white or from a working-class family is usually suppressed as irrelevant to their work role. The most significant dimension of that relationship is constituted by the *difference* between the parent and the professionals who are linked by a child: one has a parental relationship to the child, the other has specialized skills. The relationship will be affected by sex, race, and class differences but is not defined by them. Second, the right can address a universal 'parent' because we are defined as such by the state. Since the state took over education in the last century, all parents have the right and the obligation to send children to school. Third, parents are organized as a group *vis à vis* the school and are the constituency which elect parent governors. There are therefore real ways in which parents are constructed as a group by the school even though divisions and differences within that group can be just as important as elements of unity.

There is no typical experience of a parent in relationship to the school. However, one's own experience can be taken as symptomatic though not representative of experiences shared by many parents, and valuable in understanding how the right has succeeded in mobilizing parental opinion. The comments here reflect my having a 6-year-old daughter in primary school. If I face certain problems despite a job which gives me a degree of self-confidence and training in higher education, I can assume that some of these problems are experienced by others with a different background.

For me the school meets two needs: childminding and specialized education — in that order. *In loco parentis* means to me first of all that my daughter is the school's responsibility during school hours and mine and her father's at other times. Statistics and personal experience indicate that childminding is a crucial function of the school for the overwhelming majority of women. Thirty per cent of women work at least part-time even before their youngest child is at school. This rises to 62 per cent when the youngest is between 5 and 9 years old and 71 per cent if s/he is over 10 (General Household Survey Preliminary Results for 1981). It is school, therefore, which makes it easier for mothers to seek a job, although most will have no choice but to organize their working lives around school hours. For many of us the way the school day and the school year are organized is a major problem, but then so are working mothers a 'problem' for the school. The increase in mothers with young children in the workforce means that far fewer parents are 'on tap'. A school closed for half term, for use as a polling station, or for a strike disrupts parents' lives in a way that it simply did not some years ago. This childminding function goes against the grain of the professional training of teachers whose job it is to teach. Moreover, my needs as a working parent often contradict their personal needs as workers. To fulfil their own domestic responsibilities they depend on a particular organization of the working day and year.

Education is important in itself, of course. Parents feel passionately about the education of their children. Meetings on language and numbers skills at my daughter's inner-city school are always well attended — by parents from different class and ethnic backgrounds. If claims about a decline in basic skills are influential, they relate to a real concern. They connect with the high expectations of a good education and life chances for all children by a mass of parents brought up under the welfare state. The standard of judgement is not the past: we have lost all collective memory of how bad things used to be. The mass of the population is demanding more of schools than they used to.

The right's answer is to reorganize these higher expectations around a meritocratic model of individual achievement. Parents can see the inadequacies and failure of the British education system. If an elite in fact benefits unfairly from the present system in ways which remain obscure and mysterious, why not support a plan which is put forward by the right as benefiting all those with ability, whatever that means? The widespread concern about children's need to acquire basic skills relates to an awareness that those without these skills are trapped at the bottom of the heap.

In fact, schooling is a mystery to parents. However open a school, what goes on during the school day remains a blank. According to my daughter, undoubtedly protecting jealously the achievement of a separate experience, they 'never do anything'. If I were to drop in — and like most if not all parents I can't because I have a job — I'd only be a distraction. It would require considerable extra time and effort, in resource terms, plus a new attitude, for a teacher to explain the philosophy behind the methods used. I am favourably impressed with the individual treatment children receive in my daughter's school: each child has individual reading and arithmetic schemes. But this undoubtedly advanced attitude presents real problems for all parents interested in their child's schooling. In the absence of a written report, a tangible piece of paper giving the parent an assessment, however inadequate, we depend on the odd comment. How do I know what to expect, let alone whether things are on the right track? And when is it appropriate to expect more? If my child is being considered as an individual, what view of her capacity does the teacher have? Is it the same view as mine? Which is more accurate? Is there an acceptance of a stereotype or something less than 'full' potential — for whatever reason? Will I appear pushy?

Parents feel vulnerable when they talk to a teacher, because they see themselves as dependent on the latter for the child's welfare. Dependence and vulnerability hinder a positive relationship as does relating to a person simply as *professional*. The teacher must disguise he or she is a worker seeking job satisfaction, who may need support, and who is often drained by the various demands; the teacher may also be a parent. The teacher appears as someone with specialized teaching skills. But all parents 'teach' whether they realize it or not. Of course we aren't professional teachers: we aren't specifically trained and our involvement is concentrated on one or a few children over a limited period. We don't specialize in teaching. It occurs alongside everything else we do in the home and at work, but we know something about teaching. If parents complain that education can't always be fun, could it be that, through their practical experience, they feel there is a grain of truth in the saying, 'If at first you don't succeed, try, try again'?

Professionals who specialize in teaching have thus developed some of the skills we all have, however embryonically. To the extent that this expertise appears as a monopoly of knowledge, the property of the teacher, unexplained to the parent, it constitutes a barrier between parent and teacher. Just as a skilled mechanic has a better chance of fixing a car than someone who can simply use a spanner, teachers know more about teaching than parents. Defensiveness about maintaining a monopoly over skills, whether it takes an archaic professional or corporate trade union form, divides teachers from parents. There are real difficulties in overcoming this division which must be recognized if they are to be broken down. It is very difficult, for example, to explain the principles of the new maths to most of us who have learnt (badly) the old. And yet from the point of view of what parent and teacher have *in common* — an interest in the education and development of the child — an increase in parental knowledge so that parents can reinforce the educational process at home is precisely what is needed.

At the same time as asking a great deal of schools, parents are also well aware of how much children learn from other sources, in particular from television, but also from friends, babyminders, parents. Certainly most of the facts and much of the vocabulary they learn comes from television. The level of knowledge held by children today is vastly higher than when we were young. How do schools relate to that?

Neither PTAs nor school governors' meetings provide a suitable forum to talk about most of these things. The structure of consultation between parents and teachers does not permit parents to raise questions about what they feel deeply but find difficult to articulate. What may appear to teachers as a threat to their professional status needs to be confronted in the course of discussion. There is a need for debate and one of the preconditions for the success of such a debate is clarity rather than inhibitions about the *differences* between teachers and parents, between parents of different races, classes, sexes, between generations. At the moment it is usually just too embarrassing to talk about these things. If it is ever to be possible, it must be put forward as a problem to be overcome. This is the precondition of our talking about the need for compromise and considering the political question: compromise about what, for what, within which parameters? Only then can we consider how a democratic progressive politics can be created out of our differences.

That parental power, even as now organized, can be harnessed to a progressive cause has been evident, for example, in the fightback against the dismantling of the ILEA. If, on the other hand, some parents do not always go out of their way to participate in the life of the school, it probably reflects a very rational calculation about an investment of time and effort and the probable outcome. Middle-class concern is but one expression of this calculation. Elements of unity can be built around an awareness that for the vast majority of parents the state system is the only choice. If the right has been able to harness a widespread sense of dissatisfaction, the onslaught on state education of recent years can only be combated by a recognition of the reality behind this dissatisfaction in parental experience, an experience which also contains goodwill, and the hope for a better future.

15. Teachers and their organizations

Ken Jones

The most palpable changes in teachers' working lives under Thatcherism result from cuts in government expenditure. The size of classes has increased in many areas, less is being spent on books and equipment and there is less 'remedial' and nursery provision. Teachers' jobs are less secure. Although compulsory redundancy for full-time staff has been avoided (or fought off) so far, their compulsory redeployment from one school to another is on the increase. So is the use of temporary contracts. According to a survey of about half the local education authorities in England and Wales carried out by the National Union of Teachers in 1982, sixteen of them employed more than 5 per cent of their teachers on temporary contracts which the union considered unacceptable. Some LEAs employ 12 per cent of their teachers in this way.

The effect of these measures has been summed up in a report by Her Majesty's Inspectorate: 'Teachers' morale was worn very thin as the uncertainties ... arising from falling rolls and the cuts ... affect both the maintenance of present standards and the attempt to bring about improvements.'

The teachers' position in pay bargaining has been weakened as employers are able to offer a choice between pay or jobs. As a result, teachers' pay is now worth 35 per cent less in real terms than it was in 1975. The unions have tried to stop this slide by renegotiating pay-scales to enable teachers to rise to a higher point on the scale of increments without promotion. They are also trying to secure agreement on limiting the size of classes and improving 'supply' cover for absent teachers — both of which would mean more jobs. The employers have rejected all these proposals on the grounds of their 'impossible' cost, and have countered with demands for compulsory lunch-time and after-school activities. In addition, they propose to introduce forms of assessment — to be passed through before teachers could move off a basic pay-scale — and 'accelerated promotion' for certifiably 'good' teachers.

These proposals would clearly cut down teachers' control over their own work, and the idea of a merit-stream for good teachers would be more divisive than the present promotion system. Teachers would be judged not on their suitability for specific posts, but on the degree to which their work in the classroom conforms to criteria not yet defined, although presumably determined by national policy goals.

The collective voice of teachers is also losing influence in the national system of curriculum development. The Schools Council, on which the 'profession' was strongly represented, has been abolished. There is no automatic teacher representation on the separate bodies dealing with the curriculum and examination which are replacing it — they will be nominated by the Secretary of State. The planned reorganization of examinations at 16-plus, amalgamating the CSE and 'O' level boards, will weaken the impact of school-devised Mode 3 syllabuses. These have often been the most important means of progressive innovation in the fourth- and fifth-year secondary curriculum.

Not all progressive reform has been stifled by these developments since 1979. Areas of experiment remain — in some English departments, for example, where the syllabus and teaching methods are subjected to critical revision. Multi-ethnic education continues to receive attention and sponsorship. But the emphasis now is clearly on gearing education to 'the world of work' and economic needs. Even though it by-passed schools, the Youth Training Scheme has created in many of them an urgent desire to attract some of its traffic. 'Vocational' sixth-form courses are hastily being put together. The Technical and Vocational Education Initiative and Keith Joseph's offer of 'extra' money to local authorities which contrive courses for the 'bottom 40 per cent' will create similar pressures lower down the school.

These initiatives are affecting the ways that teachers themselves see educational priorities. These are still expressed in terms of 'the needs of the student', but these needs are increasingly seen to be for vocational courses. At a time of both high youth unemployment and a declining school-age population, school managements are also keen to promote them — if only to keep the number of pupils up. Scale-points and promotions will therefore be channelled in this direction.

So far there has been no coherent response from the teaching unions to this basic reordering of educational priorities. Their leaders seem less concerned with the content of the new programme than with gaining a toehold of influence within it. The NUT executive 'fully supports' the YTS and laments the MSC's decision to exclude schools from it. There is certainly disquiet about the schemes in many schools. Often, however, this is expressed as resentment of 'outside interference' or as a suspicion of vocational training based on older academic models of education which have themselves been of little value to most students. In general, the changes in the content and control of the curriculum have not inspired a rethinking of strategy by teachers whose traditional objectives have been pushed to the margins of policy.

The loss of popular confidence in teachers and schools has been harder to measure than cuts in expenditure, the loss of jobs and the growth of the MSC's power. Doubtless, it has been an important factor in the decline of teachers' influence − the Black Papers and the 'Great Debate' have had their effect. It is not that parents will not defend existing provision against cutback or closure. There are countless local examples of such action. It is more that the way educational problems are defined by the 'school-industry' lobby has now won general acceptance, at the inevitable expense of teachers' professional influence on the curriculum.

The teachers' own organizations have been much changed by the years of crisis. Traditionally, they had been divided along lines of sex and status − grammar school teachers, for example, had a separate union. Now political, or at least ideological, distinctions are steadily becoming more important. This has not entailed a general radicalization among teachers. If anything, there has been a slight numerical shift towards the unions which present themselves as 'non-political'. In the NUT, though, the left is gaining in influence.

About one-fifth of teachers in England and Wales belong to the Assistant Masters' and Mistresses' Association (AMMA) or the Professional Association of Teachers (PAT). Both forswear militancy, neither is affiliated to the TUC, and the PAT is explicitly anti-union. AMMA's membership is drawn mostly from secondary schools, as is that of the TUC-affiliated National Association of Schoolmasters/Union of Women Teachers. Originally − and still predominantly — a male union, the NAS/UWT has grown considerably over the past 20 years and now claims over 100,000 members. It has a rather undeserved reputation for militancy on basic trade union issues like pay and conditions of service. This mock-ferocity is combined with a somewhat authoritarian view of education — it espouses the idea of a crisis of discipline, for example, and advocates the retention of corporal punishment.

Along with the National Union of Teachers, these organizations are locked in competition for an increased share of a shrinking teaching force. One tactic for attracting members used by AMMA, PAT and NAS/UWT is to contrast their own 'non-political' stance against that of the NUT.

Just under half the teachers in England and Wales belong to the NUT. Nearly 60 per cent of them are women. Two-thirds teach in primary schools. Unlike the other unions, the NUT has always linked the advancement of teachers' interests with the extension of education and of equal opportunity. This background means that it is particularly sensitive to the historic break with the traditions of state education accomplished under Margaret Thatcher's government. Whereas its colleague-rivals often seem to see only an opportunity for competitive recruitment in the disarray created by cuts and restructuring, the NUT is at least engaged in a debate about strategic responses to the crisis.

This debate is superimposed upon the process of 'trade unionization' that has occurred over the past 10 years. A generation of activists influenced by the radicalism of the 1968—74 period — two teachers in every five are under 35 — has begun to assume local positions of leadership. The union's 'cadre' as a whole has become less dominated by head teachers and more familiar with trade union forms of action. Since 1979, there have been prolonged strikes in several areas: Trafford, Avon, Barking. There have been dozens of token strikes and instances of 'no cover' action. More members have been involved in action against cuts than at any time in the union's history. The build-up of local struggles is having a molecular effect on the union's leadership. At every level — from school representative to executive member — a recomposition has taken place, which has tended to promote those willing to organize action at the expense of those who lack enthusiasm for it. At national conference, 40 per cent of votes are now regularly cast for positions to the left of the executive's.

At the same time, the union has been forced to take the interests of its women members more seriously. It now recognizes that cuts have a particular effect upon women teachers, who are more likely to be on temporary or part-time contracts than men. It opposes discrimination in promotion and pay and is calling for improved maternity and paternity leave. In 1983, it held its first conference on equal opportunities for women, where most delegates were critical of the union's record.

It cannot be said, however, that such issues have yet become a central part of the union's everyday concerns. They tend to be matters for conference declarations rather than present action. Until the union's women members are fully represented on local and national leaderships, this is likely to remain the case. At the moment only five out of more than forty executive members are women.

The union's militancy, of course, has its limits. Compulsory redundancies will be fought with strikes: other cuts, no matter how damaging, with lesser measures. Local associations are disciplined if they take action without national endorsement. Nevertheless, the NUT's actions have been effective in securing their limited ends, and contrast sharply with the feebleness of other teaching unions. It is also one of the NUT's strengths that it sees its response to the educational crisis in terms that go beyond defensive and sectional trade unionism. It has tried to face up to the decline in its own influence, and to the weakening of the tradition to which it has adhered.

The union leadership conceives its present strategy as, essentially, the forceful reassertion of the principles that underlay consensus in the past — especially the idea that there is a link between increased educational opportunity for all and national prosperity. It hopes, also, to recreate the type of alliance built up around this view — an alliance that stretched from Butler to Crosland and included teachers, trade unionists, civil servants and employers. This is the aim of the union's campaign 'Our Children, Our Future', launched in mid-1983.

The difficulty that this strategy immediately confronts is the present polarization of educational debate. The union's documents rummage among the statements of Conservatives, past and present, to discover declarations of faith in state education. But although they evoke a Conservative tradition of educational benevolence they are scarcely able to point to its present vitality. The union is reluctant to face the fact that 'equal opportunity' is now more than ever a slogan of the left, not of an all-embracing alliance. Fearful of losing members, it shuns the overt political alignment which an effective struggle to reduce selection and privilege entails. Whereas many union activists wish to see the union establishing an explicit alliance with the labour movement, the leadership and its supporters would see such a break with the past as a catastrophe. Yet it is difficult to see how the conception of a recreated inter-class consensus is to find a home in Thatcher's Britain.

The traditional pillars of teacher trade unionism — political neutrality, a strong lobbying influence on government, the defence of teacher autonomy — have all been thoroughly shaken. The result has been not a widespread upsurge of radical opinion among teachers, but a shift of allegiance to the right. This has not been led by an organized 'non-political' tendency. It is *because* they opt out of any serious attempt to influence educational policy and withdraw from issues of controversy that the other unions, concerning themselves only with their limited professional interests, have attracted new members. They have no alternative strategy to propose for education.

In the growing polarization among teachers, this slight drift to the right has been matched by the growing influence of the principles of trade union solidarity and action. This has been not only in struggles around the leadership of the union, but also among teachers having to deal with immediate problems. Many have traditionally believed that teaching and militancy are incompatible. Since 1979, however, the deterioration of their conditions has led tens of thousands to become directly involved in strikes and other forms of 'industrial' action. This can involve making a fundamental decision about the nature of their trade unionism. Equally, teachers' co-operation in actions like the one-day strike in support of the health workers in 1982 can lead to a reassessment of what it means to work in 'a profession'.

Such changes of attitude are a necessary, though not a sufficient, condition for winning large numbers of teachers to more radical conceptions of educational strategy. Given the need to defend education and the position of those who work in it, it is not surprising that the 'left' advance among teachers has so far followed a path of militant trade unionism. Nor, in my view, is it a matter for regret. But if the

NUT, in particular, is to become part of a popular, critical coalition for the defence of education and for the reworking of its perspectives, then a socialist strategy within the union requires a number of changes.

The NUT can no longer operate as a professional pressure group. The introduction of YTS has made the content of the curriculum and the definition of national curricular objectives matters of political debate. The union should therefore engage at this political level. It should reject pressures towards 'education for industry', but support a curriculum based on the critical participation of students in public and productive life.

At present, the NUT's educational policy exists either as a rather diffuse ethos or in the form of presentations − committee papers, essentially − to examination boards, local authorities and the Secretary of State. The union therefore needs to take a more active lead in getting its own members to implement its policy at school level.

At the same time, it should give up its attempts to separate educational issues from social and economic policy. It is not possible that its policy would be implemented by any government other than a Labour one. The union should acknowledge that its concerns are, inevitably and properly, *political* and take part in all the debates from which it currently abstains.

Equally, it is not possible to envisage an effective Labour government unless it is one that is based on a popular movement capable of regaining and reshaping the ideological ground lost to the Tories. The NUT, like many other public sector unions, could play an effective part in such a movement − but only if it is prepared to make the nature of the 'service' in which its members work the subject of a genuine debate with those who have experience of it. Uncritical defence of an education which is said to be best left to the professionals is not likely to stir many hearts. Such a project implies, for the NUT, both a reconsideration of systems of educational control, and a practical willingness to work with those who, like black parents, have many criticisms of the system and its teachers.

Lastly, the NUT must become a union which mobilizes the consistent and active support of all its members. This requires encouraging women members, and submitting the structures, policies and practices of the union to criticism by them. This process would also entail the mobilization of the union's membership (mainly female) in primary schools. The construction of a movement of women teachers within the union is, from this point of view, an important aspect of strategy.

16. Anti-sexist initiatives in a mixed comprehensive school: a case study

Annie Cornbleet and Sue Libovitch

In the East End of London, in a mixed comprehensive school in Hackney, twelve girls sit in a classroom. A woman teacher gently directs the conversation towards their feelings about their race, their colour, their religion and their class. They begin to talk about themselves, how they feel about their bodies, their personalities, their relationships with their friends, families and teachers. In another classroom, a group of boys are doing the same thing with a male teacher.

Single-sex groups are one of the new and important outcomes of anti-sexist work, which has been in progress over a 5-year period, in Stoke Newington School. The history behind such initiatives brings out the question of how to tackle an educational system that discriminates against its pupils and staff on the basis of their class, race and sex.

Work began in 1978, when one woman teacher together with a group of 15-year-old young women wrote and produced a play entitled *It's a Hard Life Being a Girl* which was performed to both mixed and girl-only audiences. The controversy surrounding the question of the performers' rights to decide their audience highlighted basic sexist attitudes of both pupils and staff. As a result of this, a mixed anti-sexist working party was formed. The working party undertook to examine the effects of sexism in the classroom and throughout the school. This involved studying the sex-stereotyped option choices pupils were taking up, the provision made for pupils outside usual school time, the position of women teachers on the staff in relation to the men teachers, and the problem of unequal teacher time and attention being given to the boys at the expense of the girls. A report was drawn up and presented to a staff meeting, at which, after much debate and controversy, anti-sexist school policy was adopted. The report then went to the governors of the school, who acknowledged its importance and, to a certain extent, recognized the implications regarding the part they had to play within the running of the school.

In 1980, whilst teachers were criticially examining both their practice within the classroom and the resources they were using, it was acknowledged that the social behaviour of the pupils, both inside and outside lessons, was inhibiting their learning and their personal development. In order to counteract positively these problems, a single-sex Assertiveness Training Programme was introduced. This took the form of providing an environment where the students could explore the expectations placed on them because of their sex. Girl students were with women teachers and boys were with men teachers. The teachers had volunteered to work on this programme over and above their usual duties and this later proved to be a drawback in terms of the school's commitment to providing resources for further initiatives. Those teachers involved recognized that in order for the status and validity of such different ways of learning to be visible, they had to be incorporated into the body of the curriculum as a whole and not as an extra activity dependent upon goodwill. One of the most important outcomes of this programme was a marked increase in the confidence and self-esteem of the girls' groups.

During this period, a senior teacher with responsibility for anti-sexist work was appointed. This proved to be a major turning point regarding the politics of feminism and class for those women teachers involved.

Within the hierarchy of a school structure, a senior teacher cannot fail to be divided in her loyalties between the interests of management and those colleagues who are trying to initiate change. The fundamental changes that are brought about by a feminist perspective on education, are in direct conflict with the power structure of a school. To appoint an individual to a position of power tends to contradict the nature of the work and necessarily subsumes it. So during the year 1981−82 it was agreed by the staff to discontinue the senior teacher post and for the women's group collectively to take on the responsibility.

As the consciousness of the school changed, more work began in several areas of school life and what follows are some examples of successful initiatives:

Challenges to the hidden curriculum

- The creation of a girls' only space inside and outside the school building.
- Single-sex counselling.
- Single-sex tutorial times.
- Jobs' conventions — this involves consciously presenting the students with role models of people in non-sex-role stereotyped jobs.
- Working creatively with groups of girls who write and produce their own material and perform it.
- The incorporation of girls within In-service Training Courses.
- The encouragement of male teachers to work with the boys.
- Positive discrimination in the appointment of women teachers into non-stereotyped departments.

Challenges to the overt curriculum

- The creation of single-sex groups or single-sex support for subjects such as maths, physics, chemistry, social studies, English and drama.
- The writing and teaching of new resource units taught in single-sex groups in humanities and English lessons in the first year.
- The writing and creation of material for mixed-ability group work.
- The allocation of an annual budget for anti-sexist work and the setting up of a resources room for women and girls.
- Encouragement for pupils to take up non-traditional option choices and to consider non-stereotypical jobs.
- Staff policy now requires departments and pastoral teams to consider allocating resources for single-sex group work.

The DASI project

During the year 1981 — 82 a project entitled DASI (Developing Anti-Sexist Initiatives) was initiated in the two Hackney schools which became Stoke Newington School. This was a positive-action project for women teachers and girl students and was designed to broaden the range of experiences and skills offered to both boys and girls in schools.*

There were three main factors in the DASI project. First, to work with the twenty-five women teachers in both schools, who were committed to the project. Second, to work directly with boys and girls in the classroom, mostly in single-sex groups. And, third, to run a series of In-service Training Courses and organize a festival.

One of the most positive outcomes of the DASI project was the In-service Training Courses which saw the bringing together of many different women teachers. Some who had been previously isolated in their work were now able to meet, talk, and share common problems and ideas with other teachers.

The benefits of such a project were numerous. Whilst awakening ideas and encouraging a deeper understanding of the position of women and girls with the education system, it gave room to strengthen and consolidate the co-operative nature of feminist work in schools.

There is no quick way to change radically and revolutionize a system which exploits and oppresses people because of their sex, race and class. That system is organized to perpetuate the status quo, and defend itself against challenges to its own interests. Whilst there is a vicious attack on the present educational system by the Tory government, it is very hard to sustain an energetic and enthusiastic commitment to new and thought-provoking ideas. But it is those radical ideas that in the end will change not only the education process, but also the prejudiced values of mainstream society.

Whilst this article has only been able to outline the structure of work undertaken, we hope that, within its limitations, we have been able to share our strategies so that you will join us and the many other feminist teachers committed to this struggle.

---

*DASI was co-written and co-ordinated by Annie Cornbleet and Sue Sanders. It was supported by ILEA as a schools' focused inset project and by the Equal Opportunities Commission. Copies of a detailed project report and resource booklet are available, free of charge, from The Women Group, Stoke Newington School, Clissold Park, London N.16.

17. Multi-cultural education and racism

Jai Singh

Racism has been an essential element of modern capitalism. Division and exploitation of workers from the Caribbean, the Indian subcontinent and Africa has been a feature of Britain over the last 30 years. The children of these workers are beginning to come through our educational system in increasing numbers and, according to the Rampton report on children of West Indian origin, the racism inherent in the system has resulted in failure and disaffection among these children.

Many progressive teachers have attempted to counter this institutionalized form of racism by first of all trying to integrate, then assimilate, and now, 'multi-culturize' the educational opportunities offered by schools and colleges. This attempt to introduce multi-cultural education is beginning to gain momentum in schools and within some education authorities.

Multi-cultural education often includes compensatory education − teaching English as a second language, black studies, and so on. Provided multi-cultural education does not directly confront racism, it is not seen as a threat to the system and so is manageable.

Still there is very little agreement about what multi-cultural education actually means. Definitions range from 'it is good education' to a 'celebration of diversity'. This imprecision is not an accident. It is a convenient diversion that deliberately fails to recognize that the social system in this country is elitist. Any initiative in the educational sphere that is going to demand fundamental changes in the structure of society will be regarded as a temporary measure to deal with a variety of crises until economic necessity and the forces of social control feel sufficiently confident to crush the initiative.

The events at Brixton, St Pauls, Toxteth and elsewhere in Britain showed just how unprepared the state machinery was to cope with the explosion of frustration caused by years of exploitation and racism experienced by the various black groups. In spite of increased expenditure on resources for the police force and the creation of specialist paramilitary policing units, the state forces failed to deal with the street violence. One of the factors they had failed to take into account was the powerful level of support that had developed amongst different ethnic groups, based on class solidarity. The state apparatus was unable to respond to this new situation at the onset, but with the willing connivance of the media, was soon able to divide the local communities along colour lines. However, the ferocity of the explosion did cause the authorities to sit back and reflect on the situations that exposed their inadequacies. The classic diversion of the ensuing report on the unrest had the desired effect of defusing the situation. The Scarman report also recommended a small-scale commitment to ease some of the worst excesses of urban decay and unemployment. These cosmetic tinkerings cannot disguise the reality of racist exploitation.

Black children, most of whom are born in this country, are experiencing an educational system plagued by falling rolls and repeated financial cutbacks. For administrators concerned with providing an education service catering for 5- to 18-year-olds, multi-cultural education seems to be not only the answer to the obvious racism of the education system, but also a means of controlling the disaffected black youngsters in the system.

Provided that multi-cultural education is no more than a 'Cook's Tour' of ethnic food and dress, it represents no threat. Teachers and the majority of non-black parents will be prepared to allow multi-cultural education to be introduced into their schools. In this way, multi-cultural education becomes marginalized and therefore controllable. But multi-cultural education could, and indeed in some cases does, challenge the assumptions and content of traditional curricula. It can question why a largely anglo-centric curriculum is still being offered in a multi-ethnic society with a rich diversity of cultures. The most important aspect of multi-cultural education has got to be anti-racist teaching.

At the moment, multi-cultural approaches are being introduced into courses or programmes that precede public examinations. We have a situation, therefore, where a child is faced with a 2-year CSE or GCE course that bears little resemblance to some of the educational experiences of the primary and lower secondary school. It is only over the past 2 years that the Joint Matriculation Board has introduced Caribbean and African literature as part of the English literature course. The examination boards that dominate the secondary school curriculum, the universities and teachers' training colleges have yet to respond in any meaningful way to reflect the changes that the multi-cultural approach could and is creating in the classroom. For many black pupils the examination courses appear irrelevant and they feel cheated by syllabuses such as history which ignore the role and contribution blacks have made to the development of the world. This point is well made by the Rampton report.

This failure and disillusionment is reinforced by the fact that blacks experience rejection more often when searching for employment than their white counterparts. One of the 'explanations' for this discrimination is the contention that blacks lack job-specific skills and generally posses a lower level of numerical and communication skills. In an era of rapid technological change, job-specific skills are a qualification for almost permanent unemployment, and there is no evidence to support the latter contention.

Yet this is the direction of New Training Initiative debate. The number of registered unemployed in Great Britain is going to continue rising until at least 1988, according to a Treasury report to the European Economic Commission. This report projects that the unemployment rate will be in excess of 3.8 million in 1988. At present two age groups figure prominently among those registered as unemployed — those over the age of 45 and those under 25.

It is significant that in the summer of 1983 there were approximately 500,000 school leavers; thousands upon thousands have little chance of finding employment. The much discussed Youth Training Scheme (YTS) has been introduced by the government to deal with this. The importance of the scheme is that it effectively raises the school-leaving age because it requires trainees to spend a minimum of 13 weeks 'off the job' receiving some form of 'education'. The core of the 13-week course is designed to concentrate on numbers and their practical application, and 'communication'. This sounds so basic in educational terms that one wonders about the sort of education that those who designed the YTS believe is being offered by secondary schools today.

The YTS is supposed to provide vocational preparation for those 16- and 17-year-olds whose entry into the job market is 'delayed for various reasons'. These young people are expected to enter the workforce with flexible and adaptable and transferable skills. Unfortunately, every single scheme that has so far been organized is offering job-specific skills that are mainly office based. A good example is the pilot scheme organized by the Stewart Wrightson Group or the Sight and Sound scheme which includes aptitude tests and interviews. Trainees are going to be 'fitted out' with job-specific skills because they will train alongside an employer's normal intake. It would be making enormous demands on employers to expect otherwise.

As part of the New Training Initiative debate it has been suggested that vocational preparation courses be offered to those aged 14 and over. Such a suggestion is dangerous nonsense. It is dangerous because it can only provide a young person with job-specific skills and experience with machinery — especially if conducted in a small firm, school or college — that will become rapidly out of date. But more importantly it undermines the professional standards of teachers, encourages the false dichotomy of mental and manual activity, and effects far-reaching changes in the curriculum content. As with the YTS, the selection process is likely to discriminate against the blacks.

The crucial issue facing education today is its attitude towards racism. A multi-cultural curriculum with anti-racist teaching as its priority is a positive step on the road to a socially democratic society. Such an approach should:

- Place the issue of racism firmly on the school/college agenda and make time for discussion and development.
- Understand the manifestation of racism and its historical context.
- Consider how racism can and does operate within the school/college's particular circumstances.
- Analyse both conscious and 'unconscious' racist behaviour.
- Analyse individual behaviour and the practices and policies of the school/college.
- Analyse the behaviour and practices of individuals and services that are part of school/college life.
- Draw upon the experience and advice of others, including the victims of racism.

The final policy of any school or college ought to include:

- A clear unambiguous statement of opposition to any form of racism or racist behaviour.
- An explanation of the way in which the school/college intends to develop practices which tackle racism and create educational opportunities which provide the foundations for a socially democratic society.
- A clear indication of what is unacceptable and the procedures, including sanctions, to deal with any transgressions.
- A statement of how the policies and practices of the school/ college will be kept under review and evaluated.

A multi-cultural curriculum seeks to eliminate all that is anti-education — distortion, bias and prejudice. It is a positive contribution towards a socially democratic society in that it confronts racism and allows cultural diversity to flourish.

18. Parental choice and community control: the case of Croxteth Comprehensive

Phil Carspecken and Henry Miller

Conservative arguments about parental freedom and Liberal electioneering around community politics have often proved effective in winning national and local support. Their rhetoric is exposed by the story of Croxteth Comprehensive School in Liverpool. The school was legally closed by the council but, despite the opposition of the city's Liberal Party and Conservative education ministers, the local community refused to accept that decision and have kept it open.

When the decision to close the school was reported in the newspapers in November 1980, it produced quite a stir — for this story was the first local people had heard about it. A meeting was arranged to start opposition to the plan. 'It was a cold and rainy night,' recalls George Smith, Croxteth's ex-headmaster, 'yet 650 people appeared.' After the meeting, parents and teachers began a determined campaign, contacting and cajoling politicians, writing letters, leafleting, attending council meetings and demonstrating. They were not discouraged when 3 months later, in January 1981,the City Council ratified the decision to amalgamate the school with the neighbouring Ellergreen Comprehensive, 2 miles away.

Their struggle, which continued for nearly 3 years, developed through three stages. In the first, which lasted for 13 months, teachers and parents worked separately in an intensive lobbying campaign. Both groups accepted the general argument for school closures. Their protest was centred on the argument that Croxteth Comprehensive in particular should remain open. The implication, sometimes explicitly stated, was that Ellergreen Comprehensive should close instead. Within 2 weeks of the published closure plan, the teaching staff produced several carefully thought-out documents for the education committee, pointing out the superiority of the facilities in Croxteth compared to those in Ellergreen. They also argued, correctly, that

Ellergreen residents had more alternative schools to choose from than Croxteth residents. Croxteth, moreover, had a serious social need for a school which went beyond the usual educational criteria. At the end of their appeals, the teaching staff listed three alternative plans to closing the school, each of which involved a closure and amalgamation of some sort.

The parents independently argued along the same lines. Ellergreen had an inferior site, buildings and facilities; Croxteth had a greater social need for a school. This last argument quickly became the point most often mentioned by both parents and teachers. The general deprivation suffered on the estate warranted, in the words of the current secretary of the action committee 'an exception' to general closure policy.

The desolation of Croxteth is indeed dramatic. It was built during the 1950s and 1960s at the outer edge of Liverpool. Designed initially to house working-class families from the crowded dockland areas of the Mersey, 24,000 people now live there. It lies six miles from the city centre with only one bus connection. The unemployment rate is 40−45 per cent for adults, 98 per cent for school leavers between the ages of 16 and 19. There is no supermarket, only a few small shops selling essentials at exorbitant prices. The scarcity of shops is greatly resented by the community's many one-parent families (40 per cent of all families) and elderly residents, who cannot manage a trip to other areas for food. Problems of massive numbers of unemployed youth with no entertainment or other facilities are reflected in the increasing incidence of vandalism on the estate. Yet Croxteth doesn't have a police station, nor a sports centre, nor a cinema.

The housing on the estate is a mixture of tower blocks, conventional housing, 3-storey blocks of maisonettes, and patches of dilapidated, abused and vandalized structures ready for demolition. Even the homes which present a good exterior suffer from poor design and inadequate absorbing capacity. A recent health survey of the estate reveals the terrible consequences of the damp, condensation, rampant mould and the presence of such vermin as rats. Croxteth has an infant mortality rate 12 per cent higher than Liverpool as a whole, its rate of low birth weights is 16 per cent higher and its rates of respiratory illnesses and nervous diseases are well above the local average.

Hence the action committee of Croxteth Comprehensive School parents added factors of social need to the criteria of educational viability. A community already so deprived felt it had a right to have its own school, regardless of the size of the school-age population. When the closure plan was announced 'they definitely felt they were having something taken away from them,' a local community worker told us. 'I think staffing should be by need, not by number,' said a member of the action committee.

Perhaps the greatest indignation was caused by lack of consultation. A few token attempts were made after the plan's announcement and hostile reception. Letters were sent to the parents a few days after the newspaper story. Though these solicited their opinion, the response — almost unanimous rejection — was ignored. Three teachers' plans fared similarly. Councillor Storey, the chair of the Education Committee, didn't even attend the hastily organized and poorly announced 'consultation' meeting of 7 January. No parents were invited; it was described as a 'farce' by those attending.

After the council vote on 28 January, parents and teachers continued to lobby politicians. The Minister of Education at the time, Mark Carlisle, gave an encouraging interview in the spring, but after the summer riots in Toxteth, and the autumn decision to retain Toxteth's comprehensive school, it became clear that all efforts had been in vain. The official announcement came on 30 November 1981. The Secretary of State for Education approved the Liverpool City Council's plan to close Croxteth Comprehensive School. Phase one ended.

The campaign began its second phase in January 1982. While the teachers seemed to have resigned themselves to closure, the parents changed their strategy and broadened their fight to the community of Croxteth as a whole. During the previous November, a 'junior' action committee had been formed by parents of children at the Croxteth Primary School. Worried by the threatened closure of the comprehensive, they organized to prevent it. This group successfully occupied the *Liverpool Echo* newspaper offices to draw attention to their case. Soon afterwards, these two committees merged. At a public meeting early in January, the Croxteth Community Action Committee was formed.

The new committee immediately introduced more radical tactics. n three consecutive evenings in February, the Action Committee organized demonstrations to block the East Lancs Road, a major highway running along one edge of the Croxteth estate. Demonstrations continued in the city centre, blocking traffic and disrupting Education Committee meetings.

After a visit by Conservative councillors to the estate on 1 March, the Liverpool Conservative Party chose to support the school. On 3 March, the Liverpool City Council voted in favour of a Labour proposal to 'reopen' a comprehensive school in Croxteth. The proposal was carried by a majority of 31 votes. The people of Croxteth thought they had won. Energy and determination had paid off.

Phase two began its Golden Age. Thinking that the fight for the school was over, the committee concentrated on the many other social ills on the estate. They formed several subcommittees to handle issues like housing, health and the elderly. 'We'd become aware, in the fight for the school, of the many other problems of our area,' explained Cyril D'Arcy, secretary of the Action Committee.

On 11 May the community received a letter from the Education Minister, Keith Joseph. The school was to shut despite the council vote. Sir Keith refused to recognize the reversal. The city council appeared helpless.

Rather than give up, the Action Committee decided to try to change Sir Keith's mind. On 18 June two coachloads of parents went to London to lobby the Minister, who was meeting the leaders of the three political parties on the Liverpool Council to discuss education plans. Sir Keith promised to visit the school. He had a tour of Liverpool planned for July, which included several schools and the Liverpool Polytechnic. A letter was duly sent, inviting him to vist Croxteth. The reply came soon after: the minister would not be able to include Croxteth on his tour.

When Sir Keith Joseph arrived at the Liverpool Polytechnic on 13 July 1982, residents from Croxteth were there to greet him. Shocked and angry at his refusal even to visit their estate, they decided to occupy the school.

So on that Friday afternoon in July, just 3 days before the end of term and the official end of Croxteth Comprehensive, angry parents took over their school. Many teachers were sympathetic to the parents' action, but had been offered posts at Ellergreen and could not jeopardize their careers by open defiance of the Education Authority.

Teachers were allowed an hour to collect their personal belongings and leave. All educational equipment and supplies remained inside and parents fetched bedding, locks, tea-pots and food. The building was made secure, a 24-hour picket arranged.

In the 2 days following the occupation many new people who had only watched the activities of the campaign from a distance came over to see their school for the first time. Suddenly the school wasn't such an intimidating place; visits were no longer a question of nervous talks with teachers or head about the progress of their children. Neighbours who'd never known each other met for the first time and began friendships lasting to this day. Days went quickly by, days of talk and tea and card games behind 'community picket' signs. One thing was sure, the authorities wouldn't get any of the educational equipment without a struggle. But what was the next step?

The idea to run their own school didn't come immediately or easily. 'We never thought we could do it,' explained one of the members of the Action Committee, an unemployed builder with two children in the school. It was proposed first by a few of the members and agreed on only after discussion with supportive teachers from outside the community. Initially a 'pilot' summer programme was run. Volunteer teachers taught a variety of subjects to residents of all ages. It was agreed to reopen in the autumn with a full comprehensive programme.

The third phase of the campaign began when Croxteth Comprehensive opened on 20 September. There was only a handful of volunteer teachers. While 50−100 students had been expected, nearly 300 arrived, and although the staff had teaching experience, none of its members had ever administered a school before. The first seven full-time volunteer teachers included a retired deputy head, an American maths teacher, two playwrights with considerable teaching experience, an unemployed science teacher, a student at Liverpool University and a recent Cambridge graduate. They were supported by several part-time teachers. Although they came to support the struggle for a school for Croxteth, they held no common ideology except the desire to teach at this school.

The day's timetable was drawn up in a quick staff meeting just before the first period during the first week until a more permanent ~imetable could be organized. Decisions were democratically made, ~ teacher serving as co-ordinator.

At the first staff meetings, teachers and parents sat together in a semi-circle. The co-ordinator asked for volunteers to take different classes. Parents agreed to take PE lessons and games, to assist in certain rooms, or to take classes with work set by teachers. The Action Committee systematically located books and paper supplies and took them to the teachers. Two 'secretaries' sat in the main office, preparing the registers, ringing the bells for period changes, sending out press releases and advertisements for more teachers. Everyone seemed determined to make this school work — everyone, that is, except the pupils.

They were aware that this year the school was different, but weren't really sure how or why. They arrived on the first day a bit nervous and apprehensive at finding the school filled with the unexpected: parents and neighbours everywhere, television cameras, snapping photographers, journalists taping interviews and jotting down notes. New teachers who introduced themselves by their first names, took classes for nearly 2 hours on a single subject, and didn't seem particularly well prepared. It was exciting but confusing. Were teachers still really teachers? Should they be called 'Sir' or Henry? 'Miss' or Sheila? To the pupils, in the end, teachers were still authority figures, and school work was still work. All of their lives in school so far had been characterized by a struggle: pupils who could talk back or avoid work gained prestige, pupils who liked to work and learn still depended on the authority of a teacher rather than the force of their own motivation. Their parents had taken up a struggle for the right of local education with government authorities. They continued to struggle against the immediate authority of teachers.

So no 'open classrooms' were introduced. Despite the media's labels, Croxteth was not a 'free school'. That wasn't what the parents wanted. They wanted a holding operation, a school run by themselves along the traditional syllabus lines, until the government admitted its mistake and reopened the school as it had been before.

By the fifth week, a core of dedicated teachers had emerged, a 5-period day was timetabled, and classes were sorted into appropriate streams. The student population had stabilized at 150, and a reasonable range of subjects was being provided.

An attempt by the local electricity board to cut off the school's power supply had to be carried out by its management because the

TGWU electricity workers refused to co-operate. It was easily thwarted by community pickets. As winter drew on, the material difficulties of running the school intensified. The Liberal authorities refused to provide free meals or uniform grants to Croxteth's pupils. Mounting fuel bills as well as the cost of food had to be met and expenses rose to over £400 a week — an impossible figure for a community like Croxteth to find. It seemed that the school might close through financial collapse.

Meanwhile, however, Phil Knibb, the chair of the Action Committee, had been using his contacts among trade unionists and others sympathetic to the campaign to raise money. The Merseyside Trades Union—Community Liaison Committee was formed, and through its efforts funds were provided to keep the school going.

The involvement of teachers from outside the community and this creation of financial and political links with the trade union movement gave the campaign a wider perspective. This led to a change in the attitude to the closure of the neighbouring Ellergreen Comprehensive. In September 1982 Cyril D'Arcy, Secretary of the Action Committee, summarized the new view:

> Everybody with an ounce of common sense realizes the wrong decision was being made, that they'd established the school on the wrong site. But we have never said this because we consider that Norris Green, where Ellergreen is, and Croxteth or Gillmoss, were Croxteth Comprehensive is, are two separate communities. And they are both entitled to have their own local comprehensive school. We see the closure of this school as just the forefront of the large battle that is to come in the fights against cuts in education.

In Liverpool the Croxteth campaign has had a number of political effects. Some of those active in it have become involved in local Labour parties, as Labour pledged itself, both in the city and in parliament, to reopen the school. Certainly the public debate about Croxteth's need for its school has undermined the reputation of local Liberals for community politics.

In the local elections on 5 May 1983, Labour won control of Liverpool Council and immediately made clear its resolve not only to reopen Croxteth as a state comprehensive, but also to staff it on the basis of curriculum need rather than the size of the pupil roll. This could not be achieved until September 1984 at the earliest, after Liverpool's plans to reorganize its secondary education have been discussed with local communities and accepted by the Secretary of State for Education. As Sir Keith Joseph remained at the DES after the Tories' general election victory in June 1983, the council's determination to fight for sensible education policies which take account both of falling rolls and also of community needs will no doubt run into further opposition.

Meanwhile the Labour Party, the Action Committee, teachers and parents are determined to continue to provide an education for the children who are presently enrolled and for those who recently have expressed a desire to return to *their* school. Whatever the final outcome of the struggle for Croxteth, their efforts have already provided an exciting experiment in community education. Usually it is middle-class groups that manage to pressurize local education authorities into keeping particular schools open. In Croxteth a working-class community protected its own school with vigour and imagination. Helped by volunteer teachers and in a crucial alliance with local trade unions and Labour Party, they have established an important precedent for those who are genuinely concerned with community control and parental choice.

Further reading

For an analysis of Thatcherism, see Stuart Hall and Martin Jacques (eds), *The Politics of Thatcherism*, Lawrence & Wishart, 1983; for the facts and figures, *Thatcher's Britain: A Guide to the Ruins*, Pluto Press and *New Socialist*, 1983. Also Nick Bosanquet, *After the New Right*, Heinemann, 1983, especially chapter 12 on educational vouchers.

For an analysis of the 'social-democratic' consensus in education and the rise of the 'new right', see CCCS Education Group, *Unpopular Education*, Hutchinson, 1981; on the 1970s and early 1980s, John Ahier and Michael Flude (eds), *Contemporary Education Policy*, Croom Helm, 1983.

On education and training, see Pauline Brelsford, Graham Smith and Andrew Rix, *Give us a Break: Widening Opportunities for Young Women within YOPS/YTS*, MSC Research and Development series pamphlet no.11, 1982; J. Farley, 'The Great Training Robbery', *Marxism Today*, November 1982; Christine Griffin, *The Good, the Bad and the Ugly: Images of Young Women in the Labour Market*, University of Birmingham CCCS stencilled paper, 1982; Christine Griffin, *Typical Girls? The Transition from School to Un/employment for Young Working Class Women*, Routledge & Kegan Paul, forthcoming; Merilyn Moos, *Government Youth Training Policy and its Impact on Further Education*, CCCS stencilled paper, 1979.

On education and gender, see Val Amos and Pratibha Parmar, 'Resistances and Responses: The Experience of Black Girls in Britain', in Angela McRobbie and Patricia McCabe (eds), *Feminism for Girls: An Adventure Story*, Routledge & Kegan Paul, 1981; Rosemary Deem (ed.), *Schooling for Women's Work*, Routledge & Kegan Paul, 1980; Sue Sharpe, *Just Like a Girl*, Penguin, 1976; Rosie Walden and Valerie Walkerdine, *Girls and Mathematics: The Early Years*,

Bedford Way Papers/Heinemann Educational, 1982; Valerie Walkerdine, 'Sex, Power and Pedagogy', *Screen Education* no. 38, 1981.

On the curriculum, see Michael Apple, *Education and Power* Routledge & Kegan Paul, 1982; Tim Horton and Peter Raggatt (eds), *Challenge and Change in the Curriculum*, Hodder & Stoughton, 1982; Geoff Whitty and Michael Young (eds), *Explorations in the Politics of School Knowledge*, Nafferton Books, 1976. For a 'new right' view, see Roger Scruton, *The Meaning of Conservatism*, Penguin, 1981, chapter 7.

On progressive and primary education, see Harold Entwistle, *Child-centred Education*, Methuen 1970; Julian Henriques, Wendy Hollway, Cathy Urwin, Couze Venn and Valerie Walkerdine, *Changing the Subject: Psychology, Social Regulation and Subjectivity*, Tavistock, in press, chapter 4.

On discipline, moral order and the family, see Jane Coussins and Anna Coote, *The Family in the Firing Line*, NCCL/CPAG, 1981; Keith Hoskin, 'The Examination, Disciplinary Power and Rational Schooling', *History of Education*, vol.8, no.2, 1979; D.P. Leinster-Mackay, 'Regina v Hopley: Some Historical Reflections on Corporal Punishment', *Journal of Educational Administration and History*, vol.9, no.1, January 1977; B. Turner (ed.), *Discipline in Schools*, Ward Lock, 1973.

Notes on contributors

Anthony Arblaster teaches in the Department of Politics at Sheffield University

Caroline Benn teaches in adult education and has written and researched extensively on comprehensive education

Phil Carspecken, an American mathematics teacher, is a full-time volunteer at Croxteth Comprehensive School and is also working on a Ph.D

Annie Cornbleet teaches in Hackney. She has been committed to anti-sexist education for the past 8 years

Roger Dale teaches Sociology of Education at the Open University

James Donald teaches in the School of Education at the Open University and is a member of the *Formations* Editorial Collective

Jim Grealy is Head of English at Fulham Cross School, London

Andy Green, a teacher in further education, studied at the Centre for Contemporary Cultural Studies, Birmingham University

Christine Griffin is writing up the research conducted while at the Centre for Contemporary Cultural Studies, Birmingham University, and is a youth worker with young women and girls

Stuart Hall is Professor of Sociology at the Open University

Roger Harris teaches Philosophy at Middlesex Polytechnic and is active in NATFHE at local and regional level

Richard Johnson is the Director of the Centre for Contemporary Cultural Studies, Birmingham University

Ken Jones, an English teacher in a London comprehensive, is both a member of the National Executive of NUT and the Socialist Teachers' Alliance

Sue Libovitch was born, educated and now teaches in Hackney

Henry Miller, lecturer in Sociology of Education at Aston University, now teaches in the Faculty of Management and Policy Studies. The department in which he previously worked was dissolved as a result of cuts

Rick Rogers is a journalist who writes on education for the *New Statesman*, the *Guardian*, and the *Times Educational Supplement*

Anne Showstack Sassoon lectures in Politics at Kingston Polytechnic

Jai Singh is an advisory teacher in the Multi-Ethnic Inspectorate of ILEA

Valerie Walkerdine teaches and researches at the Institute of Education, University of London

Geoff Whitty teaches Urban Education at Kings College, University of London

AnnMarie Wolpe teaches Sociology at Middlesex Polytechnic and is a member of *Feminist Review* collective